Singing in Celebration

Also by Jane Parker Huber
from Westminster John Knox Press

A Singing Faith

Singing in Celebration
Hymns for Special Occasions

Jane Parker Huber

Westminster John Knox Press
Louisville, Kentucky

Book design by Jennifer K. Cox
Cover design by Kim Wohlenhaus

First edition

Published by Westminster John Knox Press
Louisville, Kentucky

This book is printed on acid-free paper that meets the American National Standards Institute Z39.48 standard. ∞

PRINTED IN THE UNITED STATES OF AMERICA

96 97 98 99 00 01 02 03 04 05 — 10 9 8 7 6 5 4 3 2 1

ISBN 0–664–25648–1 (pbk.)
ISBN 0–664–25649–X (pbk. : spiral)

For Bill, for our children, our grandchildren, and especially for Zadok (July 2–14, 1990), who already knows better than any of us how to live and sing God's praise eternally.

Contents

Preface   1

What Is Different about Writing Hymns?   5

Some Words about Words   7

Part 1. Faith and Praise

1   God of Beauty, Truth, and Grace
2   When, in Awe of God's Creation
3   Sovereign God of Every Creature
4   Christ Has Come, Salvation Bringing!
5   O God of All Creation
6   Oh Dios de lo Creado
7   We Sing Our Praise to God
8   Sing, My Soul, in Praise Unending
9   Planting Seeds of Faith and Trust
10   "God Is Love," the Bible Teaches
11   Gracious God of All Creation
12   "I Am Who I Am, I Will Be Who I Will"
13   "I Am Who I Am"—Our Living God's Name
14   Creator of Mountains

Part 2. Word and Words

15   Word of God in Human Language
16   God of All Communication
17   Words Are Tools of Peace and Justice
18   All Praise to God for Word and Words
19   We Will Sing a Song of Women
20   The Lord's My Shepherd
21   Your Word, O God, a Sharpened Blade

Part 3. Mission and Service

22   God of Time and Space and Thought
23   We Remember with Thanksgiving
24   God Is Here in Word and Action

25   O God in Christ, You Call Us into Mission
26   Loving God of All Creation
27   Holy God of All Creation
28   Holy God, We Name You
29   Seeking to Be Faithful Servants
30   Loving Spirit, Our Creator
31   Christ, You Give Us Living Water
32   Gratefully Offer Talents and Service
33   Loving Spirit, Great Creator
34   Sovereign God of All Creation
35   God beyond Us, God within Us

Part 4. Peace and Justice

36   Sing We Now of Peace with Justice
37   "Peace to You"—These Words of Jesus
38   Justice Is a Journey Onward
39   O Give God the Praise for Friendships That Last
40   O God of Earth and Altar
41   Praise the God Who Formed and Loved Us

Part 5. The Church (Past–Present–Future)

42   God of Our Years
43   God of Life, in Christ You Lead Us
44   God of Days and Years and Eons
45   O Faithful God of Years Long Past
46   God of Beginnings
47   O God, You Call to Service Day by Day
48   O Gracious God, by Whom the Church Is Founded
49   Creator God, You Build Your Church
50   Open the Doors for Christ!
51   O God, You Build the Church
52   Rejoice! Our Loving God

Comments on the Hymns   83
Index of Churches, Programs, and Individuals
   for Whom the Hymns Were Written   106
Index of Scriptural Allusions   107
Index of Composers, Arrangers, and Sources   109
Alphabetical Index of Tunes   110
Metrical Index of Tunes   111
Index of First Lines   112

Preface

When I took up the task of compiling hymns I had written since the publication in 1987 of *A Singing Faith*, I soon realized that most of my work had been at the request of a congregation or a pastor, a program of the church (denominational or ecumenical), or a planning committee for a conference. Hence the title *Singing in Celebration*. I believe the message here for the church is that we need hymns to sing for significant milestones in our lives as individuals and as congregations, hymns that sing of how we are both *special* and *connected*. The result is that even though the hymns in this collection were, for the most part, each written for a very particular, present occasion, they also speak of our faith that reaches into both the past and the future, beyond the limits of time and location.

These hymns represent my efforts to capture the ideas, projects, and celebrations of

> anniversaries of congregations and programs,
> annual themes or programs such as those in the Presbyterian
>   Peacemaking Program,
> the launching of the New Revised Standard Version of the Bible by
>   the National Council of Churches,
> the mission of the church,
> significant events such as installations, conferences, building and
>   rebuilding of churches.

A word about the arrangement of this book and the order of these hymns. Most, if not all, of the hymns in this collection could well be placed in another section of the book. The second hymn, for example, was written for the Presbyterian Peacemaking Program and might have been placed in the section on "Peace and Justice" rather than in "Faith and Praise." The arrangement presented here is meant to be helpful for those planning worship around specific themes, whether for a formal worship service or for the opening of a small group meeting.

The two introductory essays preceding the hymns may be useful as material in a workshop or a worship setting.

1

I group the hymns into five sections, as follows.

1. Faith and Praise

The focus of the first section of hymns is on God's providence and love in all of creation and all of life, with gratitude, faith, and praise as the appropriate human responses. The wonder and beauty of the earth and the solar system and the interconnectedness of all of God's creation are not new ideas, but they have renewed emphasis in current environmental concerns and in explorations of dimensions of spirituality long dormant in Reformed Christianity.

Although many favorite traditional hymns are hymns of faith and praise, there is always room for a fresh way of praising God. Hymns written with the intent of praise focus more easily on God than on the singer, thus avoiding self-centered faith, an easy pitfall of today or any day.

2. Word and Words

The second group of hymns deals with the Word, as it has come to us in scripture (notably in recent years in the New Revised Standard Version of the Bible) and in the person of Jesus Christ. These hymns also deal with the way we use words to heal or to hurt. I care so much about words that I have included a separate introductory piece, "Some Words about Words" (page 7), in which I discuss issues of inclusive language.

3. Mission and Service

Here I touch on several aspects of the church's mission today, honoring past ways of "doing mission" but pointing us toward a future of partnership and mutuality in mission. Mission hymns of the past were quite naturally concerned with getting the gospel to the whole world, sometimes with an "us-versus-them" attitude rather than one of mutual respect as children of God. Past success in spreading the Word means that we now find ourselves in mission together with Christians nearby and in other parts of the world. The comments about specific hymns deal more fully with these ideas.

4. Peace and Justice

Themes of peace and justice find their way into many of the hymns I have written, but this section highlights those written specifically for such programs in the church. As noted above, the second hymn in this book, "When, in Awe of God's Creation," could well have been placed in this section. Requests have come not only from the Presbyterian Peacemaking Program but from other denominations and ecumenical bodies as well. As people of faith, we have learned to probe deeply into issues of peacemaking: we are uncovering aspects of peace from the international to the personal; we recognize relationships among persons, and also the relationships between human beings as creatures and other created beings in the environment. This leads to inevitable connections with issues of justice.

5. The Church (Past–Present–Future)

Congregations choose to celebrate their past, present, and future in various ways. In a church development committee meeting recently, someone remarked with regret that in new hymnals there is a lack of hymns about building, rebuilding, and renewing churches. I believe the reason for this is that churches like to write or commission a hymn of their own for such occasions. (I often think I have said about all I can say about church centennials!)

Here, then, are resources for celebrations of various sorts, beginning with anniversaries and ending with building and rebuilding, "not alone by stone on stone, but grace on grace."

Following the hymns is a section of comments about each of the hymns, detailing the circumstances that led to the writing. The comments appear in the same order and with the same number as the hymn to which they refer, for easy cross-reference.

Finally, several indexes will assist in planning worship and in getting acquainted with the material in this collection.

Writing Hymns

When I am asked to write a hymn, I request background information such as church bulletins, newsletters, mission statements or themes, histories, interests, and emphases. This material helps me understand the congregation or program and its hopes for the future, as well as particular past and present characteristics and the congregation's own sense of its mission.

I also ask for suggestions for tunes. Sometimes there are several possibilities offered; sometimes there is only one requested. Often, if there is a choice, I select at least one tune in public domain, not because I dislike newer tunes, but so that copyright is not a problem for printing the music. It is no secret that congregations find it easier to sing new words to a familiar tune than to sing new melodies, even if the words are well known.

When several tunes of the same meter are familiar, some may find it helpful to print only the words in order to try various tunes suitable to the occasion. One example of this is presented in the notes for "God of All Communication" (no. 16), where I suggest four different tunes, each of which complements the words in a particular way. An example of similar texts set to different tunes—one of which requires six lines (87 87 87), the other, eight lines (as in 87 87 D)—may be found in the notes for the two hymns with similar first lines, "Loving Spirit, great Creator" and "Loving Spirit, our Creator."

When hymns are written for a particular occasion it is important that the planners of the event realize their contribution to the creative process. It is especially gratifying to me when a commissioned hymn meets the expectations and purposes of those who have requested it. Further gratification comes when hymns written for a special event take on a life of their own and find their way into general use throughout the church's life.

I pray that may happen with these words. May they be found useful in the life and mission of Christ's church, to the glory of God.

What Is Different about Writing Hymns?

Hymns are written to be part of the liturgy—the work of the people of God. When you write a hymn, you are *putting words into the mouths of other people, other worshipers.* The words of hymns become the words of a worshiping congregation. It is not helpful, in my opinion, to use this forum to introduce ideas that are going to alarm or shock or greatly distress the believer. It *is* helpful to express time-honored and time-proven truths in fresh new ways, in language and thought-forms familiar and meaningful to those who will sing the hymn. It can also be helpful to point out the connections for people between long-standing truths (biblical emphases, for example) and current ways of expressing those truths or emphases.

Incidentally, this is one of the reasons it is helpful to use tunes that people already know or that have a familiar meter and rhythm.

In contrast, when you write poetry *as poetry* (even when it may be read or recited by another person)—those are your *own* words, and sometimes *your words only.* Another person may resonate with them, may heartily agree with them, and certainly may use them in worship, either private or corporate, but hearers get to *hear* them first, rather than having them spring off the page into their own mouths.

This distinction is like the difference between a prayer written for use in *unison* and, on the other hand, a *pastoral prayer* or another prayer to be led by a single individual. In writing hymns or other liturgical materials for *congregational use,* one should not ramble too much and should avoid what I call "rabbit trails," which take a person off on a side track or a side issue, making that person lose the train of thought, or the place on the page, or even a sense of worship. There are times and places for presenting challenging ideas to disturb complacency in thinking, but if hymns are the vehicle, extraordinary care is needed.

I suppose this distinction that I make does not hold up universally! I would be surprised if it did. But consider the songs composed and performed by artists so creatively and well beginning in the 1960s and 1970s. A few of them are easily usable in many situations and by congregations, but some of the creativity almost "doesn't work" when anyone other than the composer or author sings the songs.

In fact, some hymns are *meant* to jar us, to wake us from our lethargy during liturgy. There are hymn writers who like to do this and who do it supremely well. That is not my style.

We may not know in our lifetime what will endure of today's veritable flood of hymns, but I would put my bets on hymns that are

> relevant to our time,
> suited to many different occasions of worship,
> easy to sing,
> *not* jarring,
> contemporary but not "cute."

Some Words about Words

I am a word person. I like words. They can make me laugh or cry, remember, forgive, respond with sympathy or frustration. Words make a difference, so they need to be chosen with care.

That is the reason for inclusive language. When I am challenged by people about my concern for inclusive language, I ask them to consider a grade school girl, about age ten, sitting in church today, the last part of the twentieth century. If the minister says, "God loves all men," the girl may wonder if she too is loved by God. (Even a boy may wonder if God loves him now, or only when he will grow into a man.)

The way we use language *does* change! The above illustration is not the "fault" of the children or a poor upbringing by their parents. Most of us, quite subtly, have become accustomed to language and pictures that are more gender-inclusive than those of another generation. We who are adults may never have considered our own childhood and primary education as a limited, stereotypical way to think about people; but we are only now learning not *always* to picture a man when the word "doctor" is heard or read, and a woman when the word "nurse" is used. If newscasters (note: not just newsmen!) can learn new ways of speaking, surely we can do so as we speak and sing God's praise in worship.

This brings us to the mysterious power in the words and music of worship that gets hold of us at the core of our being. Why do we cling to favorites from our childhood whether they still say what we believe or not? Can we change?

One answer may lie in the "right and left side of the brain" discussion. The *words* we sing challenge our thought; the *music* we sing hooks our emotions. Someone once pointed out to me that that was why people *can* and *do* sing my hymns: I write words that speak in a contemporary way about our faith, but mostly I use tunes that are familiar, evoking a comfortable familiarity and even tapping subliminally into the significance of the "good old" words without archaic language or outdated expressions.

When someone mentioned to me that I hooked both sides of the brain in my writing, my initial reaction was a little bit like the child who, when first hearing the hymn "Morning Has Broken," said, "But I didn't do it!" I simply, very fortunately, stumbled upon a useful blend of new and old, fresh and familiar, contemporary and traditional.

Having begun in the 1970s writing new hymns usually set to tunes of hymns that had *exclusive* language, I quickly moved to a wider variety of tunes and a broader range of concerns about language.

How and why do we limit God by using only one, or a very few, of the possible names or titles for God? If other people have *not* had an experience of a loving, supporting father, as I had, what does it mean to them to call God "Father," and never anything else? Perhaps more important still is the way in which human beings are accustomed to *picture* God in their mind's eye; if the *words* are invariably masculine in gender, a corresponding picture appears of a male figure (usually old and often bearded). Thus we lose the richness and variety of scriptural references and make God into an image acceptable to us, forgetting that God said, "I will be who I will be!"

There are, of course, *other* ways we exclude people by the words we use in worship. In working on *The Presbyterian Hymnal*, the text subcommittee learned to be sensitive to "light and dark language," in which "white" is always good and "black" or "dark" is always evil. We were led into a new understanding of how we use "light" and "dark" words and images (the white hats and the black hats!); and although we did not eliminate all light and dark language from the hymnal, we *always* thought about it and discussed whether it was language that was descriptive of "the human condition" (dark of night to dawn of day, for example), or was it *dark* (or black) as pejorative and evil, and *light* (or white) as good.

We also tried to be careful about language sounding derogatory, accusatory, or blaming about persons with handicapping conditions. It is one thing to *refuse* to see or hear; it is quite a different thing to be unable to see or hear. I confess that this is very difficult for me, because I love the sights and sounds of life so much!

We looked for hymns that include children as "real persons," and ones that do not demean advancing years—recognizing that we are not *all* in the years of prime physical strength and productivity, but we *are* all beloved children of God.

A love of words, and especially the words we use in worship, also leads to a consideration of *ideas* that are important to us today but often not encompassed in relevant hymns for use in worship. Some of the questions we must ask are:

> What *issues* are not addressed in hymns?
> What *seasons of the church year* are underrepresented in church hymnody?
> What *sacraments* and *celebrations* are short on hymns?

What new understandings of the church's *mission* need to be
expressed in hymns?

What is *happening in the church* that calls for a hymn of praise
or challenge?

These are compelling questions for me. Some are addressed in the hymns
contained in this book. The questions will always be there and new hymns
will be needed.

"Praise God, from whom all blessings flow!"

Part 1

Faith and Praise

O Lord, you are my God;
    I will exalt you, I will praise your name;
for you have done wonderful things,
    plans formed of old, faithful and sure.

Isaiah 25:1

God of Beauty, Truth, and Grace

1 God of beau - ty, truth, and grace, You have rich - ly blessed this place,
2 As the trees grow straight and tall, Soft in spring-time, bright in fall,
3 As the birds their car - ols raise, May our voic - es sing Your praise,
4 With the pass - ing of the years, Full of laugh - ter mixed with tears,

Fer - tile land and flow - ing streams, Peo - ple filled with hopes and dreams:
May our lives be strong and true, Root - ed in our faith in You.
Speak - ing words of love and cheer To Your chil - dren, far and near.
May each gen - er - a - tion show Ways to nour - ish, ways to grow.

Grant that we may hon - or You By our plans and la - bors too.
Grant that we may cher - ish here Ev - ery sea - son, ev - ery year.
Grant us qui - et, gen - tle touch When our words might be too much.
Grant us thought - ful - ness and care For each life that's here to share.

Jane Parker Huber, 1993

Words © 1996 Jane Parker Huber

DIX 77 77 77
Adapted from a chorale by Conrad Kocher, 1838

2   When, in Awe of God's Creation

1 When, in awe of God's cre - a - tion,
2 Blue and tan, with lace clouds swirl - ing,
3 Liv - ing now, this is the pic - ture
4 Now we face the un - known fu - ture,

We view earth from out - er space,
Flung in space and cir - cling there,
We no long - er can de - ny,
Chal - lenged by the work at hand.

This mys - te - rious, float - ing mar - ble,
Ha - bi - tat for myr - iad crea - tures
For we see no an - gry bound - aries
Still the God of all cre - a - tion

Strewn with clouds and bathed in grace!
Meant for land and sea and air!
When our view is from the sky:
Sum - mons us with one com - mand:

How can we not pause in won - der,
Must we draw our lines of ha - tred
Riv - ers, des - erts, for - ests, snow - fields,
"Love each oth - er!" Will we do it?

See - ing earth as one and whole,
Mark - ing land and class and race?
O - ceans, lakes, and moun - tains too,
"Love each oth - er!" Wars might cease!

Then, con - fess - ing our di - vi - sions,
God, for - give us, we en - treat You,
But no fenc - es built for bar - ring
"Love each oth - er!" Jus - tice fol - lows;

Make earth's heal - ing our prime goal.
For all pride of self and place.
You from me or me from you.
"Love each oth - er!" There is peace!

Jane Parker Huber, 1991

Words © 1992 Jane Parker Huber

HYFRYDOL 87 87 D
Rowland Hugh Prichard, 1831

3 Sovereign God of Every Creature

1 Sov - ereign God of ev - ery crea - ture, Mak - er of all things that are,
2 Shake a - way our la - zy plea - sure, Pride in ac - tions of the past;
3 In Christ's strength would we be serv - ing, Build - ing up the least, the lost.
4 So may we re - spond with vi - sion, Chal - lenged by Your glo - bal view,

Carv - er of each at - om's fea - ture, Sculp - tor of each sun and star:
Send in - stead in full - est mea - sure Deeds that wit - ness, hopes that last.
By Your grace, for - give our swerv - ing, When we hoard or count the cost.
Fear - ing not each hard de - ci - sion We must make for what is true.

We, Your peo - ple, pause in won - der, Grate - ful for Your lov - ing care.
Teach us gra - cious - ness in giv - ing, Ech - o - ing Your lav - ish hand.
Show us each how much we need You In our wor - ship, work, and play.
Lead us not in - to temp - ta - tion. Give us tasks de - mand - ing skill,

Jar us with the Spir - it's thun - der; Show us how to do and dare.
Teach us faith - ful - ness in liv - ing, Here as stew - ards of Your land.
Knit to - geth - er all who heed You, All who hear Your call to - day.
Christ our Strength and our Sal - va - tion, Christ our sure Foun - da - tion still.

Jane Parker Huber, 1989

Words © 1992 Jane Parker Huber

HYMN TO JOY 87 87 D
Ludwig van Beethoven, 1824
Arr. Edward Hodges (1796–1867), alt.

Christ Has Come, Salvation Bringing!

4

1 Christ has come, sal - va - tion bring-ing! Tell the news to ev - er - y land.
2 Sing the song and tell the sto - ry. Let our lives pro- claim God's love.
3 Christ is risen! Can you be - lieve it? Hu- man sin has done its worst.

Let us all, God's prais - es sing-ing, Reach- ing, touch - ing, lend a hand.
All cre - a - tion shouts God's glo - ry, Deep- est seas to skies a - bove.
Here's the good news; just re - ceive it! Here is quench - ing for our thirst.

Let the gos - pel proc - la - ma - tion Sound from shore to dis - tant shore,
But the won - der of all won-ders: "God is with us!" each and all.
Christ is ris - en! Death, de - feat - ed! Life, re - stored in full - est power!

Ech - o back the ex - cla - ma - tion, "Sin is van - quished ev - er - more!"
God for - gives our thought- less blun - ders, Picks us up each time we fall.
And that tri - umph is re - peat - ed Day by day and hour by hour.

Jane Parker Huber, 1987

FABEN 87 87 D
John H. Willcox, 1849

Words © 1996 Jane Parker Huber

5

O God of All Creation

1 O God of all cre - a - tion—Of earth and sea and sky,
2 But we who are Your crea - tures Re - ject our crea - ture-hood
3 Where we have spoiled cre - a - tion With self - ish - ness or waste,
4 In con - fi - dence we come now. Your truth has set us free
5 So, God of all cre - a - tion, Who formed and called it "good"

Of cac - tus, shrub, and red - woods, Of beasts that creep and fly—
And fail to make this plan - et A glo - bal neigh-bor - hood.
Or squan-dered earth - ly trea - sures Through care - less - ness or haste,
To work for peace and jus - tice And earth's in - teg - ri - ty.
To be di - verse and col - or - ful, A glob - al neigh-bor - hood,

The sweep of light and col - or, The range of shape and size
Re - store to us the vi - sion. Your im - age print a - new
Cor - rect us and chas - tise us, In - struct and clar - i - fy.
We stand with - in cre - a - tion, Re - lat - ed, in - ter - twined
Re - form us in - to kin - ship With crea - tures great and small,

Com - mand our ad - o - ra - tion And stun us with sur - prise!
On us who need new mod - els Of ways to think and do.
O Christ, we need for - give - ness. Re - deem us or we die!
With for - ests, seas, and crea - tures Of blood and bone and mind.
With broth - er rain and sis - ter wind, With sun and stars and all.

Jane Parker Huber, 1990

Words © 1992 Jane Parker Huber

LLANGLOFFAN 76 76 D
Welsh folk melody
Evans' *Hymnau a Thonau*, 1865
As in *English Hymnal*, 1906

Oh Dios de lo Creado

6

1 Oh Dios de lo cre - a - do, En tie - rra, cie - lo y mar,
2 No - so - tros Tus cria - tu - ras Al nues - tro ser ne - gar.
3 Si la crea - ción da - ña - mos, Con e - go - ís - mo tal,
4 Con fe en Ti ve - ni - mos, Li - bres por Tu ver - dad,
5 Oh Dios de lo cre - a - do, Quien di - jo, "Bue - no es"

De cac - tus, yer - ba y ro - bles, A - ves en su vo - lar,
No ha - ce - mos del pla - ne - ta La ve - cin - dad glo - bal.
Que los te - so - ros da - dos, Per - da - mos sin cui - dar.
Pa - ra lo - grar jus - ti - cia Y paz, in - te - gri - dad.
Que a to - dos nos hi - cis - te Dis - tin - tos, mas ya ves,

Luz y co - lor a - dor - nan, Y to - da la crea - ción.
Res - táu - ra - nos Tu i - ma - gen, Y da - nos la vi - sión
Co - rrí - ge nues - tras fal - tas, En - se - ña - nos a a - mar.
De Tu crea - ción hoy so - mos, U - na u - ni - dad vi - tal.
Re - for - ma Tus cria - tu - ras, De nue - vo haz nos sen - tir,

A a - do - rar - te in - vi - tan Con gran ad - mi - ra - ción.
Pa - ra ob - te - ner mo - de - los Nue - vos de fe y ac - ción.
Oh Cris - to, Te pe - di - mos Per - dón pa - ra en Ti es - tar.
Con bos - ques, ma - res, se - res Da - nos a - fi - ni - dad.
U - ni - das con la llu - via, Con Tu crea - ción fe - liz.

Jane Parker Huber, 1990
Trans. Ana Inés Braulio-Corchado

Words © 1996 Jane Parker Huber

LLANGLOFFAN 76 76 D
Welsh folk melody
Evans' *Hymnau a Thonau*, 1865
As in *English Hymnal*, 1906

Faith and Praise

7   **We Sing Our Praise to God**

1 We sing our praise to God Who made the earth and sky, All
2 We sing our thanks to God For years of lov - ing care, For
3 And still we sing our praise, To - day as in the past, For

flowers and trees and grow - ing plants, All things that run or fly,
church and home, for work, for friends With whom to dream and dare.
God has led us to this hour With strength and love that last.

All peo - ple, large or small, Sun, moon, and stars so bright, For
In grat - i - tude we sing, Re - call - ing days gone by, While
And Christ has made us one With peo - ple ev - ery - where, A

God is God of all that is, Of dark - ness and of light.
look - ing for - ward joy - ful - ly With hopes and spir - its high.
world- wide hu - man fam - i - ly With whom to grow and share.

Jane Parker Huber, 1990

TERRA BEATA SMD
Franklin L. Sheppard, 1915

Words © 1996 Jane Parker Huber

Sing, My Soul, in Praise Unending

8

1 Sing, my soul, in praise un-end-ing: Just and righ-teous
2 God has called us to be loy-al Stew-ards of both
3 God in-tends us for re-lat-ing, Rec-on-cil-ing,
4 Sing to God with spir-its leap-ing, For our God makes

are God's ways. Now with oth-er voic-es blend-ing, Swell-ing sound shall
word and deed, Trust-ing each as neigh-bor roy-al, Meet-ing ev-ery
mak-ing peace, Car-ing e-ven while de-bat-ing, That our lis-tening
all things new, Mold-ing, shap-ing, prun-ing, keep-ing, Re-cre-at-ing

sing God's praise. Al - le-lu - ia! Al - le-lu - ia!
hu - man need. Al - le-lu - ia! Al - le-lu - ia!
nev - er cease. Al - le-lu - ia! Al - le-lu - ia!
peo - ple too! Al - le-lu - ia! Al - le-lu - ia!

Praise be-gins and ends our days. Praise be-gins and ends our days.
Love and jus-tice form our creed. Love and jus-tice form our creed.
Jus - tice in the world in - crease. Jus - tice in the world in-crease.
There's a world of hope in view. There's a world of hope in view.

Jane Parker Huber, 1987

Words © 1996 Jane Parker Huber

CWM RHONDDA 87 87 877
John Hughes, 1907

9 Planting Seeds of Faith and Trust

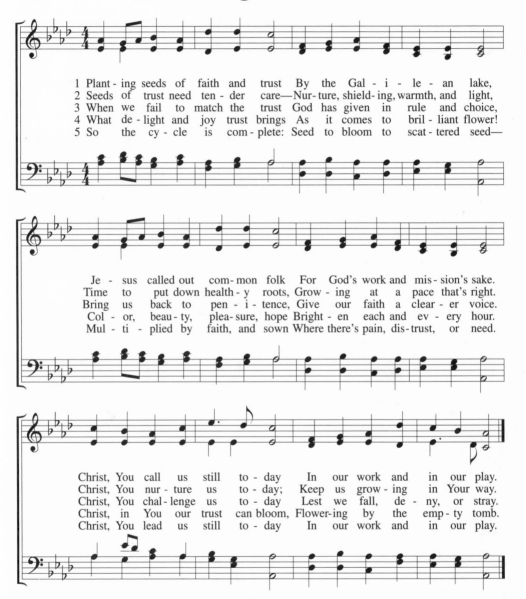

1 Plant-ing seeds of faith and trust By the Gal-i-le-an lake,
2 Seeds of trust need ten-der care—Nur-ture, shield-ing, warmth, and light,
3 When we fail to match the trust God has given in rule and choice,
4 What de-light and joy trust brings As it comes to bril-liant flower!
5 So the cy-cle is com-plete: Seed to bloom to scat-tered seed—

Je-sus called out com-mon folk For God's work and mis-sion's sake.
Time to put down health-y roots, Grow-ing at a pace that's right.
Bring us back to pen-i-tence, Give our faith a clear-er voice.
Col-or, beau-ty, plea-sure, hope Bright-en each and ev-ery hour.
Mul-ti-plied by faith, and sown Where there's pain, dis-trust, or need.

Christ, You call us still to-day In our work and in our play.
Christ, You nur-ture us to-day; Keep us grow-ing in Your way.
Christ, You chal-lenge us to-day Lest we fall, de-ny, or stray.
Christ, in You our trust can bloom, Flower-ing by the emp-ty tomb.
Christ, You lead us still to-day In our work and in our play.

Jane Parker Huber, 1987

DIX 77 77 77
Adapted from a chorale by Conrad Kocher, 1838

Words © 1996 Jane Parker Huber

"God Is Love," the Bible Teaches

1 "God is love," the Bible teach-es; Yes! God is love!
2 E - ven though we might for-get it, Still God is love.
3 God is love! Now we re-peat it, Yes! God is love!

Peo - ple say, and our church preach-es, Our God is love.
Do you think God might re - gret it? No! God is love!
There's no news that can de - feat it! Yes! God is love!

We, too, sing of love un-end-ing, All our voic-es clear-ly blend-ing,
God is faith-ful night and day-time, In our work and in our play-time,
We raise up our voic-es sing-ing; We can al-most hear bells ring-ing,

Now to you the mes - sage send-ing, "Yes! God is love!"
Jan - u - ar - y, March, and May-time. Yes! God is love!
Joy - ful - ly the good news bring-ing, "Yes! God is love!"

Jane Parker Huber, 1987

Words © 1996 Jane Parker Huber

AR HYD Y NOS 84 84 88 84
Traditional Welsh melody
Harm. by L. O. Emerson, 1906

11

Gracious God of All Creation

1 Gra - cious God of all cre - a - tion, Your will be done.
2 Faith - ful God of all cre - a - tion, Your will be done.
3 Lov - ing God of all cre - a - tion, Your will be done.

In our joy and cel - e - bra - tion, Your will be done.
Keep us true to our vo - ca - tion; Your will be done—
Bless and hal - low each re - la - tion; Your will be done.

Help us in our learn - ing, grow - ing; May we feel the joy of know - ing
Here with You our cov - enant seal - ing, Here Your hol - y pres - ence feel - ing,
You have made our lives for shar - ing, Life - af - firm - ing, tend - ing, car - ing.

Won - ders of the Spir - it flow - ing. Your will be done.
Our com - mit - ment now re - veal - ing, Your will be done.
When we come, our love de - clar - ing, Your will be done.

Jane Parker Huber, 1989

Words © 1996 Jane Parker Huber

AR HYD Y NOS 84 84 88 84
Traditional Welsh melody
Harm. by L. O. Emerson, 1906

"I Am Who I Am, I Will Be Who I Will" 12

1 "I am who I am, I will be who I will,
Un - fet - tered Cre - a - tor and cre - a - ting still!"
In such words of free - dom, our God's clar - ion voice
Speaks loud - ly or soft - ly, and our hearts re - joice.

2 "I am who I am!" now in this time and place.
God with us! Christ with us! the full - ness of grace!
Each day is ex - cit - ing, with jus - tice our goal,
The Spir - it ig - nit - ing new flames in the soul.

3 "I am who I am!"—God both faith - ful and free;
Un - bound by tra - di - tion, "I'll be who I'll be."
"I will be who I will be"— God be - yond thought,
Un - shack - led by an - y - thing peo - ple have wrought.

4 God's names are so var - ied: Rock, Ea - gle, and Dove,
Mes - si - ah, Em - man - u - el, Wis - dom, and Love.
Yet all are re - flec - tions of on - ly a part.
"I will be who I will be"— that is the heart!

Jane Parker Huber, 1995

Words © 1996 Jane Parker Huber

ST. DENIO 11 11 11 11
Welsh folk melody
Adapted in *Caniadau y Cyssegr*, 1839

13 "I Am Who I Am"—Our Living God's Name

1 "I am who I am"— our liv - ing God's name;
2 "I was who I was" in fire or in cloud,
3 "I will be who I will be," God has said,
4 So how do we praise this God who is free,

God with us in Christ, both dif - ferent and same.
In dry bones or Ark or plumb line or shroud,
The One who sets free, the One who has led.
Who tells us, "I will be who I will be"?

So hu - man in teach - ing and feel - ing our pain, But
In part - ing or calm - ing the wa - ters of seas, "I
Un - bound - ed by i - dols of what - ev - er kind— Of
When words fail, at - tempt - ing God's won - der to trace, The

trans - form - ing death in - to liv - ing a - gain.
was who I was" and I am who I please.
met - al, clay, wood, pen and ink, or of mind.
Spir - it sur - rounds us with notes full of grace.

Jane Parker Huber, 1995

LYONS 10 10 11 11
Attr. to Johann Michael Haydn (1737–1806), alt.

Creator of Mountains

14

1 Cre - a - tor of moun - tains, of gla - ciers and streams,
2 Cre - a - tor of peo - ples and rac - es and tribes,
3 Cre - at - ed for car - ing for all hu - man need,
4 Cre - a - tor of ri - ver and for - est and snow,
5 Great God, now we come, our hearts grate - ful for days

Great Splash - er of foun - tains and Dream - er of dreams,
Not bound by church stee - ples or what myth de - scribes,
We seek to be dar - ing in thought and in deed.
E - ter - nal Life - giv - er whose pres - ence we know,
When faith, like a drum - beat, keeps stead - y our praise.

We gath - er in won - der and praise for Your grace.
We cel - e - brate now our di - ver - si - ty here,
Turn us from all strife that de - means or di - vides.
Your voice is re - sound - ing in storm, wind, and wave.
In song and re - joic - ing hopes stir and a - rise,

Re - spond - ing, we pon - der our work in this place.
In pen - i - tence vow to ac - cept and not fear.
Re - form us for life that em - powers and a - bides.
Your love is a - bound - ing, em - brac - ing to save.
Our spir - its now voic - ing their hymns to the skies.

Jane Parker Huber, 1987

Words © 1996 Jane Parker Huber

ST. DENIO 11 11 11 11
Welsh folk melody, 1839
Adapted in *Caniadau y Cyssegr*

Part 2

Word and Words

In the beginning was the Word, and the Word
was with God, and the Word was God. . . .
And the Word became flesh, and lived among us,
. . . full of grace and truth.

John 1:1, 14

Word of God in Human Language 15

1 Word of God in hu - man lan - guage For this time and in our tongue,
2 Ev - ery - where the world is hun - gry For the lib - er - a - ting Word,
3 So God's voice con - tin - ues speak - ing In the words we can't de - ny,

Tell a - new the age - less sto - ry, Ev - er an - cient, ev - er young.
Food for spi - rit as for bod - y, To be tast - ed, felt, and heard.
Sound - ing out a - cross the ag - es. Will we an - swer or de - fy?

May our hearts re - ceive the mes - sage Of God's faith-ful, lov - ing care;
It is thus the Word en - coun - ters At God's own ap - point - ed hour,
As the call be - comes still clear - er, Wit - ness that the Word shall last,

May our lives re - spond in ac - tion, Liv - ing deed and liv - ing prayer.
Bring-ing knowl-edge and per - cep - tion Of true jus - tice, peace, and power.
May we fol - low with com - mit-ment In the pres - ent as the past.

Jane Parker Huber, 1989

BEECHER 87 87 D
John Zundel, 1870

Words © 1992 Jane Parker Huber

16

God of All Communication

1 God of all com - mu - ni - ca - tion—
2 Liv - ing Word in Christ ap - pear - ing,
3 Mov - ing Spir - it, in - spir - a - tion
4 Words to - day are cheap and man - y,

Speech and sign and print - ed word—
Made more real in flesh and bone,
Of the sto - ry - tell - ers' art,
Used for ends both good and ill.

May we in this cru - cial mo - ment
Speak a - gain in phrase and ac - cent
Of his - to - rians' ear - nest rec - ord,
How we need Your Word for liv - ing

Lis - ten, that Your voice be heard.
We can un - der - stand and own,
Of each priest's and sing - er's part,
With its words that heal and fill!

Ban - ish all dis - tract - ing nois - es
Words more tru - ly those once spo - ken
Still in - spir - ing new trans - la - tion,
God, we praise You for the mes - sage

Lur - ing us to turn a - way.
In an an - cient tongue and age.
You work through the schol - ar's pen,
You have giv - en us to share,

Clear our fo - cus, help us lis - ten
Bring to life the proph - ets' preach - ing
So that we may read and pon - der,
As You of - fer, now as al - ways,

For Your Word in this our day.
And the mar - tyrs' her - i - tage.
Here to - day as there and then.
Liv - ing words to an - swer prayer.

Jane Parker Huber, 1989

BLAENHAFREN 87 87 D
Welsh melody

Words © 1992 Jane Parker Huber

17 Words Are Tools of Peace and Justice

1 Words are tools of peace and jus - tice,
2 God's cre - a - tive Word en - liv - ens
3 May our words re - flect the im - age

Tru - ly spo - ken and per - ceived, Rec - on -
All re - al - i - ty we know, Out of
Of our God's cre - at - ing power, Bring - ing

cil - ing, heal - ing, teach - ing, Lib - er - at - ing
cha - os calls forth or - der, Thoughts to cul - ti -
jus - tice and re - demp - tion So that peo - ple

when be - lieved. Do we speak by voice or
vate and sow. We are crea - tures of God's
thrive and flower— Spo - ken word and Word In -

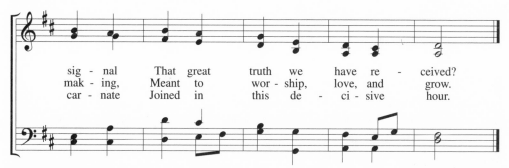

sig - nal   That great   truth we   have re - ceived?
mak - ing,   Meant to   wor - ship, love, and   grow.
car - nate   Joined in   this de - ci - sive hour.

Jane Parker Huber, 1987

LAUDA ANIMA 87 87 87
John Goss, 1869

Words © 1996 Jane Parker Huber

All Praise to God for Word and Words   **18**

1 All   praise to   God for   Word and words, For   mean-ing clear and   deep,
2 All   prais - es,   too, for   those who write, Il - lu - mi - na - ting   well
3 To   God the glo - ry   and the thanks For   schol - ars and for scribes,
4 May   we with joy both   read and hear God's Word to us to - day,

For   lan - guage that ex - press - es thought, For phras - es hearts can   keep.
Both text and con - text, word and phrase, So   all may read and   tell.
For   all who trans - late, print, and send The Word to lands and tribes.
And grate - ful - ly re - ceive and live Its   mes - sage and its   way.

Jane Parker Huber, 1989

ST. ANNE CM
Attr. to William Croft, 1708

Words © 1992 Jane Parker Huber

19 We Will Sing a Song of Women

1 We will sing a song of wom-en, young and old,
2 Sa - rah, Ha - gar, Le - ah, and the wife of Lot,
3 Han - nah was a wom - an faith-ful through the years,
4 Deb - orah judged in Is - rael, do - ing what God said.

5 First on Eas - ter morn - ing at the emp - ty tomb,
6 Nym - pha wel - comed Chris-tians; Phoe-be helped Saint Paul.
7 So we sing a song of wom-en, young and old,

Wom - en who were faith - ful, as the Bi - ble told,
Shiph - rah, Pu - ah, Zip - porah, oth - ers we for - got—
Pray - ing to have chil - dren, beg - ging God with tears.
Es - ther saved the Jews when Ha - man wished them dead.

Fright - ened wom - en won - dered what could cheer their gloom.
There was mer - chant Lyd - ia; Ma - rys, great and small.
Wom - en who were faith - ful, as the Bi - ble told.

Of - ten o - ver - shad - owed, lost, or just de - nied.
Some are named and val - ued, oth - ers all un - known;
When her prayers were an - swered, Sam - uel was her son.
Ruth left home and coun - try for Na - o - mi's sake.

Who'd be - lieve their sto - ry? "Christ a - live and well!"
Ju - lia and Pris - cil - la, Ju - nia too, we're told,
Of - ten o - ver - shad - owed, lost, or just de - nied,

We re - mem - ber them with grat - i - tude and pride.
Yet they lived by faith and wor - shiped God a - lone.
She re - joiced and prom - ised that God's will be done.
Dai - ly they would seek God's will to un - der - take.

They were first to know it— what good news to tell!
Led and served the ear - ly church with men of old.
We re - mem - ber them with grat - i - tude and pride.

Faith - ful men and wom - en, faith - ful girls and boys,

Sing and live the praise our lov - ing God en - joys.

Jane Parker Huber, 1989

Words © 1996 Jane Parker Huber

ARMAGEDDON 11 11 11 D
German melody
Adapted by John Goss, 1871

20

The Lord's My Shepherd

1 The Lord's my Shep - herd; I'll not want For
2 Of qui - et wa - ters I drink deep. The
3 Though shades of death en - com - pass me And
4 My Shep - herd e - ven spreads a feast, In
5 My cup is full, and more than full, Such

an - y - thing that's need - ed. My bed is made in
Lord re - stores my be - ing And guides in paths of
dan - ger hov - ers near me, The rod and staff my
spite of foes who'd harm me, And soothes my head with
lav - ish love out - pour - ing That I will live each

pas - tures green. All I re - quire is heed - ed.
right - eous - ness, My soul from e - vil free - ing.
Shep - herd holds Will com - fort, save, and cheer me.
heal - ing oil. What fear could now a - larm me?
night and day My Shep - herd Lord a - dor - ing.

Para. Jane Parker Huber, 1988

DOMINUS REGIT ME 87 87
John Bacchus Dykes, 1868

Words © 1990 Jane Parker Huber

Your Word, O God, a Sharpened Blade   21

Unison

1 Your Word, O God, a sharp-ened blade,
2 Cor-rect and change the words we say
3 O God of jus-tice, save us all

Cuts through the veils of hu-man sin.
When we ex-clude, de-mean, di-vide.
From an-y bit-ter, kill-ing word,

Re-move in-jus-tice! Clear a-way
Give us fresh lan-guage, clean and free,
And make our voic-es in-stru-ments

All pride of gen-der, race, or kin!
Where-in Your Spir-it can re-side.
Through which Your voice is new-ly heard.

Jane Parker Huber, 1987

DEO GRACIAS LM
"The Agincourt Song," England, c. 1415

Words © 1996 Jane Parker Huber

Part 3

Mission and Service

The Spirit of the Lord is upon me . . .
  to bring good news to the poor . . .
  to proclaim release to the captives
    and recovery of sight to the blind,
  to let the oppressed go free,
  to proclaim the year of the Lord's favor.

Luke 4:18–19

God of Time and Space and Thought

22

1 God of time and space and thought, Cre - a - tion sings Your worth.
2 God in Christ, You are our guide, Com - pan - ion on life's way,
3 Ho - ly Spir - it, pres - ent still, Wher - ev - er paths may lead,
4 Tri - une God of ev - ery time, Our chal - lenge is Your call.

Ev - ery-thing Your hand has wrought Speaks won - der to the earth.
Lead-ing peo - ple to Your side, To - day as yes - ter - day.
Mold our ac - tion and our will To meet our neigh-bor's need.
Give us moun-tains, hills to climb, And tasks both great and small.

Peo - ple called to be a part Of Your mis-sion and Your dream
Grant that we may fol - low too: Men and wo - men long a - go,
Near or far, through-out our life, May we wel-come ways to serve,
Show us fron - tiers You or - dain. We'll pi - o - neer in love to - day,

Heed the chal-lenge and take heart To join the ser - vant stream.
Heard Your call and an - swered You, Their love and faith to show.
O - ver-com-ing fear and strife. Grant pa - tience, strength, and nerve.
March, as with a wag - on train, And fol - low Christ, the Way.

Jane Parker Huber, 1993

Words © 1993 Jane Parker Huber

AMSTERDAM 76 76 77 76
James Nares (1715–1783)
The Foundery Collection, 1742

23 We Remember with Thanksgiving

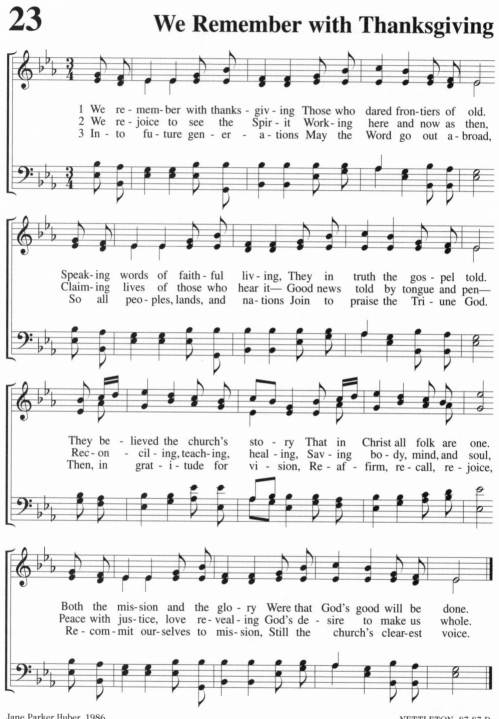

1 We re - mem- ber with thanks - giv - ing Those who dared fron-tiers of old.
2 We re - joice to see the Spir- it Work- ing here and now as then,
3 In - to fu - ture gen - er - a - tions May the Word go out a - broad,

Speak- ing words of faith - ful liv- ing, They in truth the gos - pel told.
Claim- ing lives of those who hear it— Good news told by tongue and pen—
So all peo- ples, lands, and na- tions Join to praise the Tri - une God.

They be - lieved the church's sto - ry That in Christ all folk are one.
Rec - on - cil - ing, teach-ing, heal - ing, Sav - ing bo - dy, mind, and soul,
Then, in grat - i - tude for vi - sion, Re - af - firm, re - call, re - joice,

Both the mis-sion and the glo - ry Were that God's good will be done.
Peace with jus- tice, love re - veal- ing God's de - sire to make us whole.
Re - com- mit our- selves to mis- sion, Still the church's clear-est voice.

Jane Parker Huber, 1986

NETTLETON 87 87 D
Wyeth's *Repository of Sacred Music*, 1813

God Is Here in Word and Action

24

1 God is here in word and ac - tion. God was here be - fore we came.
2 Long a - go the call to mis - sion Stirred the hearts of those who heard,
3 Still to - day, we hear the sum - mons: "Go and heal" and "preach good news."
4 Chris - tians, join in cel - e - bra - tion, Heart to heart and hand in hand!

All cre - a - tion sings God's glo - ry; Let us join and do the same.
Men and wom - en with a vi - sion Of a life based on God's Word.
May we hear and heed and fol - low In the paths that God may choose.
Teach each oth - er new di - men - sions, Al - ways true to God's com - mand.

God in Christ is our sal - va - tion; Grate - ful hearts re - spond with praise,
Fac - ing toil and sep - a - ra - tion, They em - barked on paths un - known
God grant grace and per - se - ver - ance, And the wis - dom to dis - cern
Round the world the news is spread - ing: "Christ is ris - en! Come and see!"

Liv - ing lives of faith - ful ser - vice, In the full - ness of our days.
With a mea - sure of re - demp - tion, Sure, by faith, they were God's own.
Where and how to be most faith - ful To the Christ from whom we learn.
All cre - a - tion joins the cho - rus, Now and through e - ter - ni - ty.

Jane Parker Huber, 1993

RUSTINGTON 87 87 D
C. Hubert H. Parry, 1897

Words © 1996 Jane Parker Huber

25 O God in Christ, You Call Us into Mission

1 O God in Christ, You call us in-to mis-sion;
2 Long years a - go, Your faith-ful peo-ple fol - lowed
3 O God in Christ, You call us in-to ac - tion.

In ev - ery age Your ser-vants rise and go,
When, by Your call, they trav-eled paths un - trod.
New forms of mis - sion chal-lenge and re - new.

Chal - lenged to love, to heal and teach with vi - sion,
May we, like them, show faith and pur - pose hal - lowed,
Make clear the call to u - ni - ty from fac - tion

Sure of the pres - ence of the Christ we know.
True to our call, our Sav - ior, and our God.
So, near or far, our work gives praise to You.

Jane Parker Huber, 1993

CONSOLATION (Mendelssohn) 11 10 11 10
Felix Mendelssohn (1809–1847)

Loving God of All Creation

1 Lov-ing God of all cre-a-tion, Hear our hymns of grate-ful praise:
2 Grant us cour-age for the pres-ent, Match-ing that of yes-ter-day,
3 Still to-day You call for work-ers True to Christ, the ser-vant Lord,

We give thanks for calls to wit-ness, And to serve in var-ied ways.
When Your faith-ful ser-vants ven-tured On a dis-tant, un-known way.
Shar-ing val-ues, blend-ing cul-tures; Thus new mis-sion is ex-plored.

Show us how to be con-nect-ed To Your church in ev-ery place.
We, to-day, have un-known path-ways, Far a-way and near at hand.
Through the gos-pel's ur-gent mes-sage You con-nect us, land to land,

Prais-ing Christ in lives of ser-vice, Make us in-stru-ments of grace.
Grant us ears and hearts to lis-ten For Your lov-ing, clear com-mand.
Build-ing bridg-es, span-ning chasms, Join-ing peo-ple, hand in hand.

Jane Parker Huber, 1993

Words © 1996 Jane Parker Huber

HYMN TO JOY 87 87 D
Ludwig van Beethoven, 1824
Arr. Edward Hodges (1796–1867), alt.

27

Holy God of All Creation

1 Ho - ly God of all cre - a - tion, God of hope for
2 Where, O God, in all cre - a - tion Is the chance to
3 All a - round us rise new prob-lems: Moun-tains move, foun -
4 In be - gin - ning, You cre - a - ted Har - mo - ny and
5 Lov - ing God of hope and prom-ise, Guide us to that

hu - man-kind, In the midst of change and cha - os
start a - new? Earth-ly powers that long have flour-ished
da - tions shake, Peo - ple wan - der, chil - dren scat - ter,
all things good. We have failed to keep the pro - mise,
longed-for day When Your chil - dren live to - geth - er

Grant us peace of heart and mind; And we pray for
Still hold sway in all we do. What would be a
Earth is poi - soned, cit - ies quake. Re - cre - ate us,
Stand - ing now where oth - ers stood. Help us find Your
In a just and peace-ful way, Free to find our

great - er wis - dom Than, with - out You, we can find.
glob - al sys - tem Built on faith and love for You?
God of glo - ry, For our own and oth - ers' sake.
new cre - a - tion— Make the world a neigh - bor - hood!
true vo - ca - tion Where we live and work and pray.

Jane Parker Huber, 1991

Words © 1992 Jane Parker Huber

REGENT SQUARE 87 87 87
Henry Thomas Smart, 1867

Holy God, We Name You

1 Ho - ly God, we name You God in ev - ery age,
2 Dwell - ing place and shel - ter, food for hun - gry folks,
3 To - kens we may of - fer can - not match Your gift,
4 Live - ly Ho - ly Spir - it, where You lead, we go,
5 How then can we praise You, God the Three in One?

Pres - ent, past, and fu - ture, God of his - tory's page.
Faith - ful friend and help - er shar - ing heav - y yokes,
God - head ful - ly hu - man, wea - ry hearts to lift.
E - ven when we fal - ter, wan - der to and fro.
Words are shal - low ves - sels if the deed's not done.

In the cit - y's cri - ses, You, our guid - ing power,
In the Christ, as mod - el, show us how to be
Make of us Your a - gents, rec - on - cil - ing all,
Bring us back to free - dom by Your lov - ing grace.
Voic - es soar in sing - ing Your e - ter - nal worth—

Call us to com - pas - sion in each pres - ent hour.
Ser - vants in Your house - hold, now re - deemed and free.
Prov - ing faith through jus - tice, heed - ing Your clear call.
Spring us in - to ac - tion in this time and place.
So words, deeds, and mu - sic sound Your praise on earth.

Jane Parker Huber, 1989

KING'S WESTON 11 11 11 11
Ralph Vaughan Williams (1872–1958)

29

Seeking to Be Faithful Servants

1 Seek - ing to be faith - ful ser - vants, Do - ing mis - sion
2 With all peo - ple who are strug - gling In o - be - dience
3 All a - round us God's cre - a - tion, Roll - ing sea to
4 When in mis - sion we are faith - ful, In Christ's strength we
5 Seek - ing to be faith - ful ser - vants, Do - ing mis - sion

in Christ's way, We turn to God's liv - ing pres - ence,
to God's will, We will stand and work and suf - fer,
fleck of dust, Sings, "The earth is God's pa - vil - ion!"
are made new, And, u - nit - ed in com - mit - ment
in Christ's way, We turn to God's liv - ing pres - ence,

One in Spir - it as we pray, One in Christ and
Tak - ing care to lis - ten still, One in Christ and
We, as stew - ards, must be just, One in Christ and
Learn what God re - veals as true, One in Christ and
One in Spir - it as we pray, One in Christ and

one with neigh - bor In God's world for this our day.
one with neigh - bor, Live Christ's mis - sion, live God's will.
one with neigh - bor, Share in peace the sa - cred trust.
one with neigh - bor, We learn from each oth - er too.
one with neigh - bor, In God's world for this our day.

Jane Parker Huber, 1989

REGENT SQUARE 87 87 87
Henry Thomas Smart, 1867

Loving Spirit, Our Creator

30

1 Lov - ing Spir - it, our Cre - a - tor, Gra - cious Sav - ior,
2 Grant us, in our in - ward jour - neys, Depth of in - sight,
3 When You call us for new ser - vice Through com - mu - ni -
4 May our min - is - tries and mis - sion Stretch our vi - sion

ho - ly God! We who wor - ship and a - dore You
calm of heart, Flower - ing spir - its, strength of pur - pose,
ty or church, May our full re - sponse be joy - ful
pole to pole, Reach - ing out - ward, reach - ing in - ward,

Stand in awe on hal - lowed sod. How we need Your
Lis - tening souls (prayer's pur - est art!). As dis - ci - ples,
In our la - bor, love, and search. Keep us fo - cused,
Touch - ing bod - y, heart, and soul. Bar - riers fall - ing,

new di - rec - tion To re - claim the path we've trod!
and as stew - ards, Grant the will to do our part.
strong, yet self - less, Both as per - sons and as church.
peo - ple car - ing, One - in - God our per - fect goal.

Jane Parker Huber, 1992

REGENT SQUARE 87 87 87
Henry Thomas Smart, 1867

Words © 1996 Jane Parker Huber

31   **Christ, You Give Us Living Water**

1 Christ, You give us liv - ing wa - ter, Quench-ing thirst of
2 Bap - tized once with pure, fresh wa - ter, Freed from sin and
3 Now in bread and wine You of - fer Life that does not
4 So may we, as Christ's dis - ci - ples— Men and wom-en,

tongue and heart. Teach us how to share that wa - ter,
called by grace, We who claim the sign as Chris - tians
fear to die. Are we read - y now to fol - low
old and young— Give the world life - giv - ing wa - ter,

Show us how to do our part. As You knelt with
Stand as part - ners in one place. Wa - ter is the
With - out ask - ing where or why? When we share the
Quench-ing thirst of heart and tongue: Thus to build a

cloth and ba - sin, Wash a - way our cares and pride;
en - trance sym - bol, Seal - ing what God's love be - gan,
bread and chal - ice, Serv - ing neigh - bors near at hand,
church of ser - vice Set on Christ, the cor - ner-stone;

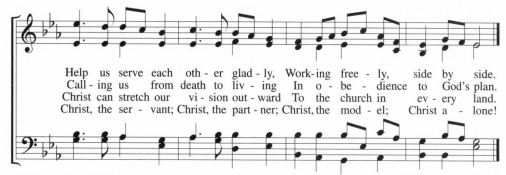

Help us serve each oth-er glad-ly, Work-ing free-ly, side by side.
Call-ing us from death to liv-ing In o-be-dience to God's plan.
Christ can stretch our vi-sion out-ward To the church in ev-ery land.
Christ, the ser-vant; Christ, the part-ner; Christ, the mod-el; Christ a-lone!

Jane Parker Huber, 1991

AUSTRIAN HYMN 87 87 D
Franz Joseph Haydn, 1797

Words © 1996 Jane Parker Huber

Gratefully Offer Talents and Service 32

Unison

1 Grate-ful-ly of-fer tal-ents and ser-vice, Meet-ing the
2 Faith-ful-ly serv-ing all of God's chil-dren, Tell-ing our
3 Joy-ful-ly prais-ing, learn-ing, sup-port-ing, Find-ing new

chal-lenge of this new day. Part-ners in mis-sion, work-ing with
stor-ies, lis-tening to theirs, Teach-ing, up-hold-ing, with love en-
paths of ser-vice and prayer, Led by the Spir-it, life we in-

vi-sion, Strength-en Christ's bod-y in a new way.
fold-ing, We help to bear all bur-dens and cares.
her-it, Giv-ing God glo-ry now ev-ery-where.

Jane Parker Huber, 1988

BUNESSAN 10 9 10 9
Gaelic melody
Arr. Dale Grotenhuis, 1985

33   Loving Spirit, Great Creator

1 Lov - ing Spir - it, great Cre - a - tor,
2 Grant us, in our in - ward jour - neys,
3 When You call us for new ser - vice
4 May our min - is - tries and mis - sion
5 Lov - ing Spir - it, great Cre - a - tor,

Gra - cious Sav - ior, ho - ly God!
Depth of in - sight, calm of heart,
Through com - mu - ni - ty or church,
Stretch our vi - sion pole to pole,
Gra - cious Sav - ior, ho - ly God!

We who wor - ship and a - dore You
Flower - ing spir - its, strength of pur - pose,
May our full re - sponse be joy - ful
Reach - ing out - ward, reach - ing in - ward,
We who wor - ship and a - dore You

Stand in awe on hal - lowed sod.
Lis - tening souls (prayer's pur - est art!).
In our la - bor, love, and search.
Touch - ing bod - y, heart, and soul.
Stand in awe on hal - lowed sod.

We would move in new di - rec - tions,
As dis - ci - ples— Christ our Teach - er—
Keep us fo - cused, strong yet self - less,
Peo - ple work - ing, lov - ing, shar - ing,
Now we of - fer all our tal - ents

An - swer - ing Your clar - ion call.
And as stew - ards of Your grace,
Dar - ing paths un - trod be - fore,
Build - ing bridg - es, clear - ing space—
To the ser - vice of Your will.

Jour - ney with us; keep us faith - ful
Grant us wis - dom, faith, and cour - age
Delv - ing deep be - yond the sur - face
Find - ing in our mu - tual ser - vice
Guide us in Your love and wis - dom;

Stew - ards of Your love for all.
For our time and in this place.
Of each chal - lenge to its core.
Christ in ev - ery hu - man face.
Where You lead, we fol - low still.

Jane Parker Huber, 1992

Words © 1996 Jane Parker Huber

HYFRYDOL 87 87 D
Rowland Hugh Prichard, 1831

34   **Sovereign God of All Creation**

1 Sov - ereign God of all cre - a - tion,
2 Lov - ing Christ, our ser - vant Mas - ter,
3 Ho - ly Spir - it, Hope of mor - row,

Reign - ing o'er all time and space,
Sav - ior of all hu - man - kind,
Ad - vo - cate for all the lost,

With us in our cel - e - bra - tion
Liv - ing with us, friend and pas - tor,
Com - fort in all pain and sor - row,

Of each mile - stone, age, and place:
Serv - ing God with heart and mind:
Faith - ful One who counts not cost:

Chal - lenge us to faith - ful liv - ing
Show us where the need is strong - er;
May Your pres - ence so in - spire us

In our day, so fraught with greed.
There our en - er - gies em - ploy.
That we feel what oth - ers feel.

As You give, may we be giv - ing
Grant us skill and pa - tience long - er
May Your flame of love so fire us

As we see our neigh - bor's need.
To ful - fill our tasks with joy.
That through us is love made real.

Jane Parker Huber, 1988

HYFRYDOL 87 87 D
Rowland Hugh Prichard, 1831

Words © 1996 Jane Parker Huber

35 God beyond Us, God within Us

1 God be-yond us, God with-in us, Ho-ly God whose praise we sing:
2 In this time of chang-ing pat-terns, New re-la-tion-ships, new hope,
3 Send us out to serve with jus-tice So, for-giv-en and set free,
4 Called to live-ly praise and wit-ness Where we live and work and play,

When You call to faith and ser-vice Take our lives as of-fer-ing.
Send a rain-bow full of prom-ise With its fo-cus, depth, and scope.
We can act with joy and heal-ing With Your Spir-it's en-er-gy.
May we of-fer love and learn-ing, Hope and nur-ture day by day.

Time and cul-ture, age and dif-ference, Add en-rich-ment to the whole.
In Your Word we find di-rec-tion From the past, yet press-ing on.
Show us how to ease the suf-fering Of our neigh-bors far and near.
Help us lis-ten to each oth-er, Our com-mu-nion to in-crease,

Called and chal-lenged, we Your peo-ple Seek a vi-sion of Your goal.
Christ, the One led by the Spir-it, Bids us face a new day's dawn.
Teach us how to work as part-ners Where the need may next ap-pear.
Giv-ing sub-stance, time, and tal-ent To our dreams of faith and peace.

Jane Parker Huber, 1992

HYMN TO JOY 87 87 D
Ludwig van Beethoven, 1824
Arr. Edward Hodges (1796–1867), alt.

Part 4

Peace and Justice

What does the Lord require of you
    but to do justice,
    and to love kindness,
    and to walk humbly with your God?

Micah 6:8

Sing We Now of Peace with Justice

1 Sing we now of peace with jus - tice, Life a - bun- dant, God's in - tent, All cre - a - tion held in bal - ance, Sea be - low to fir - ma - ment: Peace with jus - tice! Peace with jus - tice! Striv - en for, yet heav - en - sent.

2 Where there's hun - ger, drought, or fam - ine, Where earth's chil - dren drift and roam, Grant us grace to help each oth - er Live in love as in one home: Peace with jus - tice! Peace with jus - tice! Health and heal - ing, true sha - lom.

3 Where the waste of hu - man war - fare Mur - ders, in - jures, and de - stroys, Where the guns and bombs of ha - tred Shat - ter hopes with deaf - ening noise: Peace with jus - tice! Peace with jus - tice! O God, grant us wis - dom, poise!

4 So we sing of peace with jus - tice As we gath - er for the Feast, World-wide shar - ing bread and chal - ice Of - fered e - ven for the least: Peace with jus - tice! Peace with jus - tice! Each to oth - er, friend and priest.

Jane Parker Huber, 1988

LAUDA ANIMA 87 87 87
John Goss, 1869

Words © 1996 Jane Parker Huber

37 "Peace to You"—These Words of Jesus

1 "Peace to you"— these words of Je - sus Raise our hopes for
2 Peace will nev - er be dis - cov - ered While the hun - gry
3 Roads to peace are of - ten rock - y, Chal - leng - ing our
4 "Peace to you!"— A call to ac - tion, Not a sen - ti -

peace on earth. Peace!— the mes - sage sung by an - gels
go un - fed. Peace re - mains a dim il - lu - sion
ver - y soul. "Christ, our Peace" must be our watch - word;
men - tal phrase; Peace e - ras - ing ev - ery bar - rier,

Her - ald - ing our Sav - ior's birth. Peace!— the res - ur -
Till each child has home and bed. If our sys - tems
Christ, the path - way; Christ, the goal. Wheth - er in - ner
Un - der - gird - ing all our ways. "Peace," Christ's re - sur -

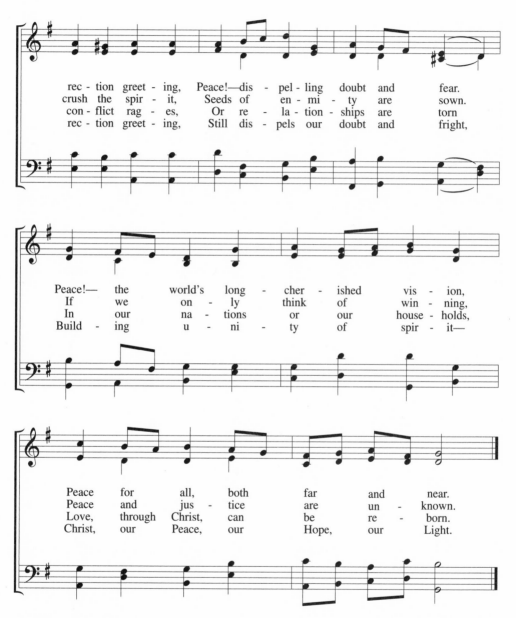

rec - tion greet - ing, Peace!—dis - pel - ling doubt and fear.
crush the spir - it, Seeds of en - mi - ty are sown.
con - flict rag - es, Or re - la - tion - ships are torn
rec - tion greet - ing, Still dis - pels our doubt and fright,

Peace!— the world's long - cher - ished vis - ion,
If we on - ly think of win - ning,
In our na - tions or our house - holds,
Build - ing u - ni - ty of spir - it—

Peace for all, both far and near.
Peace and jus - tice are un - known.
Love, through Christ, can be re - born.
Christ, our Peace, our Hope, our Light.

Jane Parker Huber, 1994

Words © 1995 Jane Parker Huber

IN BABILONE 87 87 D
Dutch melody
Arr. Julius Röntgen (1855–1933)

38

Justice Is a Journey Onward

1 Jus - tice is a jour - ney on - ward, Up - ward e - ven
2 When we hear a cry for jus - tice From the depths of
3 Em - pa - thy with - out firm ac - tion Turns to emp - ty
4 Jus - tice is a jour - ney on - ward, Up - ward, out - ward,

through the pain. Jour - neys have their hills and val - leys,
hu - man need, Our re - sponse puts love in ac - tion,
sen - ti - ment, But the call to free God's peo - ple
spread - ing still. Christ has set us on this jour - ney,

Still the dreams and goals re - main. We are peo - ple
Fol - low - ing our Sav - ior's lead. Where we see op -
Leads to self - de - vel - op - ment. When the struc - tures
Claim - ing us for God's own will. Let us share our

freed from bond - age By our Mak - er's will and power.
pres - sive sys - tems, Peo - ple hun - gry, crushed by fear,
need re - shap - ing, Or our neigh - bor is down - cast,
neigh - bor's bur - dens Far a - way or face to face.

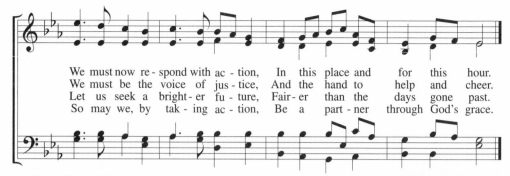

We must now re - spond with ac - tion, In this place and for this hour.
We must be the voice of jus - tice, And the hand to help and cheer.
Let us seek a bright - er fu - ture, Fair - er than the days gone past.
So may we, by tak - ing ac - tion, Be a part - ner through God's grace.

Jane Parker Huber, 1994

AUSTRIAN HYMN 87 87 D
Franz Joseph Haydn, 1797

Words © 1996 Jane Parker Huber

O Give God the Praise
for Friendships That Last

39

1 O give God the praise for friend - ships that last, For pow - er - filled
2 When in - jus - tice seems to crowd out our cause, When prej - u - dice
3 Give thanks to God, then, in times good or ill, For wom - en and

days, both pres - ent and past, For vic - to - ries won in the
schemes to make prog - ress pause, Then ral - ly the forc - es of
men, our faith - ful part - ners still, Who nev - er for - sake us what-

face of our foes, For tri - umphs of spir - it and cour - age that grows.
jus - tice and truth, For God gives us wit and the vig - or of youth!
ev - er the plight, And stand with us, firm - ly up - hold - ing the right!

Jane Parker Huber, 1987

HANOVER 10 10 11 11
Attr. to William Croft (1678–1727)
A Supplement to the New Version of the Psalms, 1708

Words © 1996 Jane Parker Huber

Peace and Justice

40   O God of Earth and Altar

1 O God of earth and al - tar, Bow down and hear our cry;
2 From all that ter - ror teach - es, From lies of pen and voice,
3 A - wak - en us to ac - tion And forge us in - to one,

Our earth - ly rul - ers fal - ter, Our peo - ple drift and die;
From all the eas - y speech - es That make our hearts re - joice,
De - fy - ing sect and fac - tion; O God, Your will be done!

The walls of gold en - tomb us, The swords of scorn di - vide;
From sale and prof - a - na - tion Of hon - or and the sword,
Op - pres - sive sys - tems snare us; Our ap - a - thies in - crease.

Take not Your thun - der from us, But take a - way our pride.
From sleep and from dam - na - tion, De - liv - er us, good Lord!
Great God, in mer - cy spare us For jus - tice and for peace!

Stanzas 1–2, Gilbert Keith Chesterton, 1906
Stanza 2 alt. Jane Parker Huber, 1985
Stanza 3, Jane Parker Huber, 1985

Stanza 3 © 1985 Jane Parker Huber

LLANGLOFFAN 76 76 D
Welsh folk melody
Evans' *Hymnau a Thonau*, 1865
As in *English Hymnal*, 1906

Praise the God Who Formed and Loved Us 41

1 Praise the God who formed and loved us,
Forms, re-forms, and loves us still,
Shows to us the whole cre-a-tion
Meant to do the Mak-er's will.
Peace with jus-tice! Peace with jus-tice!
May we each our task ful-fill.

2 Church-es, schools, and so-cial sys-tems
Hear the cries of hu-man need:
Peo-ple home-less, chil-dren drift-ing,
Hun-ger, ill-ness, war, and greed.
Peace with jus-tice! Peace with jus-tice!
When will we their groan-ings heed?

3 Peo-ple, seek-ing to be faith-ful,
Hear God's call to work and prayer.
We stand with them, heart and shoul-der,
Free to la-bor, free to care.
Peace with jus-tice! Peace with jus-tice!
Free to live, God's love to share.

4 Liv-ing, pray-ing, plan-ning, work-ing,
E-qual part-ners in God's sight,
Cul-tures, rac-es, young and ag-ing,
Wom-en, men—seek truth and right.
Peace with jus-tice! Peace with jus-tice!
In God's new cre-a-tion's light.

5 As we strive to work to-geth-er
For the whole cre-a-tion's good,
May we claim the art of mak-ing
All the world a neigh-bor-hood.
Peace with jus-tice! Peace with jus-tice!
All God's world a neigh-bor-hood.

Jane Parker Huber, 1989

LAUDA ANIMA 87 87 87
John Goss, 1869

Words © 1996 Jane Parker Huber

Part 5

The Church (Past–Present–Future)

> They called the church together and related all that God had done with them, and how [God] had opened a door of faith . . .
>
> *Acts 14:27*

God of Our Years

1 God of our years, from our birth to our life's cul-mi-na - tion,
2 God of our past, You have led us in ev-er-y en-deav - or.
3 God of to - day, e - ven now You con-tin-ue to lead us.
4 God of the fu-ture and ev-er-y new day's gen-er-a - tion,

Hear now our praise and our an-thems of glad cel-e - bra -
You of-fer heal-ing to bind what we thought-less-ly sev -
By word and deed, through Your church, You are pres-ent to feed
Stead-fast and true, You lead on to a bright des-ti - na -

tion. Through all our years, Through all our joys and our
er. When, in our pain We cry for whole-ness a -
us. In Christ, our Friend, We know Your grace with-out
tion. O - pen our hearts! O - pen our minds for fresh

tears, You come in Christ's rev-e-la - tion.
gain, You stand be-side us for-ev - er.
end; Show us where Your chil-dren need us.
starts! Fill us with new in-spi-ra - tion.

Jane Parker Huber, 1993

LOBE DEN HERREN 14 14 4 7 8
Stralsund *Ernewerten Gesangbuch*, 1665
Harm. *The Chorale Book for England*, 1863

Words © 1993 Jane Parker Huber

43 God of Life, in Christ You Lead Us

1 God of life, in Christ You lead us,
2 God of words and Word In - car - nate,
3 God of mu - sic, psalms and an - thems,
4 God of days and years and e - ons,

Guid - ing us a - long the way.
Words that chal - lenge and em - brace,
Help us sing our faith a - new:
Still You call, as in the past.

In our past, through joys and sor - rows,
Grant us bold - ness in our speak - ing,
Mel - o - dies ex - pand - ing wor - ship,
Work un - done de - mands our la - bor;

You have been our strength and stay.
While we know Your lov - ing grace.
Har - mo - nies en - rich - ing too.
Jus - tice yearns for peace at last.

Jane Parker Huber, 1992

ABBOT'S LEIGH 87 87 D
Cyril V. Taylor, 1941

44 God of Days and Years and Eons

1 God of days and years and e - ons, All our times are by Your grace;
2 God of mo - ments, hours, and dec - ades, Al - ways pres - ent ev - ery day,
3 God of fu - ture gen - er - a - tions, Still cre - a - ting all things new,
4 God of pres - ent, past, and fu - ture, All our years are in Your care;

In the past, through change and chal - lenge, You have led us to this place.
Through Your church in lov - ing nur - ture We are guid - ed in Christ's way.
Prob - ing where in - jus - tice lin - gers And up - build - ing what is true.
Men and wom - en, young and ag - ing, Join in grat - i - tude and prayer.

Hear our hymns of glad thanks - giv - ing For foun - da - tions firm - ly laid,
Hear our grate - ful prayers and prais - es For Your prov - i - dence and care.
Act to strength - en weak en - deav - ors; Move in Your mys - te - rious way;
Where we see Your pur - pose clear - ly, Where we hear Your clar - ion call,

Faith of ev - ery gen - er - a - tion— Strong ex - am - ple, pres - ent aid.
Teach us ways to tell the sto - ry; Help us to re - ceive and share.
Wake us, stir us in - to ac - tion; Speak to - mor - row as to - day.
Grant us faith to trust and fol - low, As Christ lived, for each and all.

Jane Parker Huber, 1993

Words © 1993 Jane Parker Huber

HYMN TO JOY 87 87 D
Ludwig van Beethoven, 1824
Arr. Edward Hodges (1796–1867), alt.

O Faithful God of Years Long Past   45

1 O faith-ful God of years long past And faith-ful still to-day,
2 Show us our mis-sion for to-day, O God of gra-cious power.
3 To - day we cel - e - brate and sing, Re - call-ing work well done.
4 Our grat - i - tude now o - ver-flows In ser - vice and in praise.

We praise You for all things that last A - long this earth-bound way:
We pray for vi - sion lest we stray Or fail You in this hour.
But more, we look a - head to bring To har - vest work be - gun.
The love we share still builds and grows In strong - er, deep - er ways.

For strong com - mu - ni - ties of faith, For friend-ships long and true,
So keep our fo - cus sharp and clear, Our pur - pose one with Yours,
With - out Your pres - ence sure and strong, We can - not move a - head.
So neigh-bor-hoods and cit - ies here, And na - tions near and far,

For all the joys of life and breath In Christ made ev - er new.
Till all the world, both far and near, Will know Your grace en - dures.
Your Spir-it lifts us with a song; By Christ we're loved and fed.
Will see in us Your love made clear By what we do and are.

Jane Parker Huber, 1989

WEYMOUTH CMD
Theodore P. Ferris, 1941

46

God of Beginnings

1 God of beginnings, Losses and winnings,
2 God of our testing, God of work and resting,
3 God of all mystery, God of all history,

God of the signs along the way:
Teacher and Guide on all life's road:
God clearly seen in Jesus Christ:

Show us our task, our goal, Lead us and
You ease our burden's weight, Daily, wipe
We claim that mystery, Confess that

make us whole, Walk with us still in this new day.
clean our slate, And help us bear our common load.
history, Redeemed and loved by that same Christ.

Jane Parker Huber, 1988

Words © 1996 Jane Parker Huber

CRUSADERS' HYMN 56 85 58
Silesian folk song
In *Schlesische Volkslieder*, Leipzig, 1842

O God, You Call to Service Day by Day

47

1 O God, You call to ser-vice day by day,
2 Make us one peo-ple, striv-ing toward Your will,
3 Call us to wid-er fields of work to do
4 So may our lives re-flect our faith in You,

Your pres-ence felt when in Christ's name we pray.
In faith-ful work, though bear-ing bur-dens still.
In cit-y, na-tion, and the whole world through.
Joy-ful and free, and ded-i-cat-ed too.

Be with us now, in this most joy-ful hour,
Bind us to-geth-er in Your lov-ing care,
Grant us a vi-sion of Your world at peace;
Bless now this church and peo-ple by Your grace,

As we move for-ward by Your grace and power.
As we move for-ward, led in deed and prayer.
As we move for-ward, may that dream in-crease.
As we move for-ward, in our time and place.

Jane Parker Huber, 1992

Words © 1996 Jane Parker Huber

TOULON 10 10 10 10
Adapted from Genevan 124
Genevan Psalter, 1551

48

O Gracious God,
by Whom the Church Is Founded

1 O gra - cious God, by whom the church is found - ed,
2 God of all time, all space, all love, all know - ing,
3 Lead us, O God, in - to the un - known mor - row;
4 God, grant us vi - sion bold e - nough for ac - tion.

Call us a - new to ser - vice and to praise.
With grate - ful hearts we sense Your pres - ence here.
With You as guide, we have no need to fear.
God, grant us faith, a - live, se - rene, and sure.

As we re - call the roots in which we're ground - ed,
Love leads us now to pen - i - tence and grow - ing;
Christ is the proof You share our joy and sor - row;
God, grant us friends, true part - ners, free from fac - tion.

Chal - lenge us now to mis - sion for these days.
Christ, in for - give - ness, of - fers hope and cheer.
Christ, the as - sur - ance You are al - ways near.
God, grant us work to do, strength to en - dure.

Jane Parker Huber, 1988

WELWYN 11 10 11 10
Alfred Scott-Gatty, 1902

Creator God, You Build Your Church

49

1 Cre - a - tor God, You build Your church In earth - ly space and time.
2 The walls we ded - i - cate to - day Are sym - bols of Your will,
3 May truth and love the stan - dards be For those who la - bor here,

With - out You, fruit - less is our search; With You comes grace sub - lime.
Sur - round - ing all we do and say Your pur - pose to ful - fill.
So friend - ship, chal - lenge, hope may see Their full fru - i - tion clear.

We pray Your pres - ence and Your grace Will make our vi - sion grow,
May doors and win - dows wel - come light, Re - flect - ing back the same;
May jus - tice reign with - in each hall And, hand in hand with peace,

So, spread - ing to and from this place, Good news will o - ver - flow.
May words here spo - ken bring in - sight And glo - ry to Your name.
In - form, di - rect, and chal - lenge all, Christ's mis - sion to in - crease.

Jane Parker Huber, 1988

ELLACOMBE CMD
Gesangbuch der Herzogl. Wirtembergischen

Katholischen Hofkapelle, 1784

50

Open the Doors for Christ!

1 O - pen the doors for Christ! Let light shine ev - ery - where,
2 O - pen the doors for Christ! God's chil - dren all are we:
3 O - pen the doors for Christ! The world of need a - waits;
4 O - pen the doors for Christ! O Ho - ly Spir - it, come!

To wel - come here old friends and new For wor - ship, song, and prayer.
In nurs - ery, class - room, work - place, home, In age or in - fan - cy.
May we not close our minds or hearts To those out - side the gates.
With speech on fire, and rush - ing wind, And or - gan pipe, and drum!

Our hearts fling o - pen too, Our minds and wills as well,
Seek paths of faith and truth; May learn - ing nev - er cease,
We see the work to do. God, give us strength and will
In - spire us to move on Where fu - ture doors swing wide,

That all who see us know our God, And hear good news to tell.
Till all the world's a neigh - bor - hood Of love and hope and peace.
To car - ry out Your per - fect plan With cour - age and with skill.
To tell the world a Sav - ior's love Means God is at our side.

Jane Parker Huber, 1990

DIADEMATA SMD
George Job Elvey, 1868

Words © 1996 Jane Parker Huber

O God, You Build the Church

51

1 O God, You build the church In earth - ly time and space;
2 From ash - es we a - rise, Our spir - its soar-ing free,
3 We look a - head with hope, Re - ly - ing on Your care,

Yet not a - lone by stone on stone, But grace on grace.
Since Christ has called us to the work Of min - is - try.
For Your re - deem-ing prov - i - dence Is ev - ery - where.

You tem - per us by fire With Your re - fin - er's skill,
May we re - spond in faith, With tal - ent, word, and deed,
Your work-place is the world; May we be build-ers too,

To give re - sil - ien - cy and strength To do Your will.
Wher - ev - er You may chal - lenge us Through hu - man need.
When, Spir - it - guid - ed, led by Christ, We build with You.

Jane Parker Huber, 1990

LEONI (YIGDAL) 66 84 D
Traditional Hebrew melody

52

Rejoice! Our Loving God

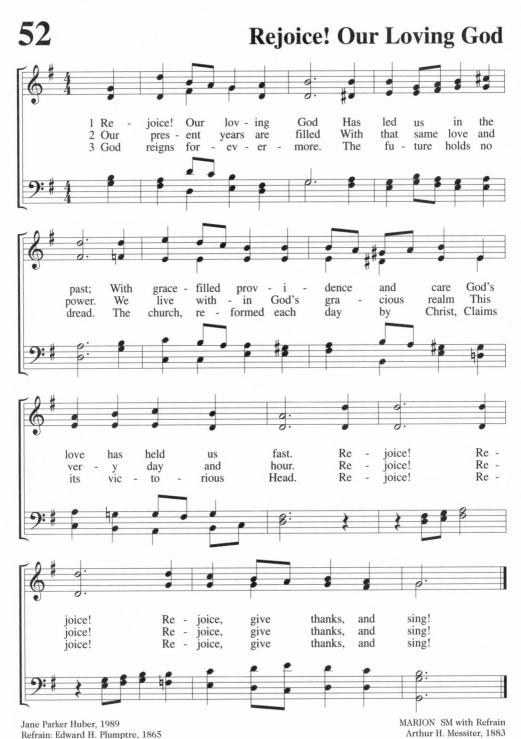

1 Re - joice! Our lov - ing God Has led us in the
2 Our pres - ent years are filled With that same love and
3 God reigns for - ev - er - more. The fu - ture holds no

past; With grace - filled prov - i - dence and care God's
power. We live with - in God's gra - cious realm This
dread. The church, re - formed each day by Christ, Claims

love has held us fast. Re - joice! Re -
ver - y day and hour. Re - joice! Re -
its vic - to - rious Head. Re - joice! Re -

joice! Re - joice, give thanks, and sing!
joice! Re - joice, give thanks, and sing!
joice! Re - joice, give thanks, and sing!

Jane Parker Huber, 1989
Refrain: Edward H. Plumptre, 1865

MARION SM with Refrain
Arthur H. Messiter, 1883

Words © 1996 Jane Parker Huber

Comments on the Hymns

1   God of Beauty, Truth, and Grace

This hymn of praise was written for Englishton Park Presbyterian Ministries, Inc., since the 1950s a residence for older people, and since 1970 uniquely combined with a remarkable summer program for children.

Englishton Park is at the edge of the small southern Indiana town of Lexington, on 665 acres of farmland and woods. In its heyday it had been a country estate, and its manor house became the first residence for retired persons attracted to a rural setting. The manor house is gone, having been replaced by a two-story brick residence (accommodating couples or singles) with a common dining room and lounges. Thirty to forty-five places are available, depending on double or single occupancy, and there is also space on the property for building a small retirement home of one's own. My mother very happily spent her last seventeen years there.

The summer program recently celebrated twenty-five years of an intensive camping program for children who are bright but doing poorly in school because of various problems such as low self-esteem or a very negative attitude toward people and school. The camp was conceived in the mind of Harve Rawson, professor of psychology at nearby Hanover College, as a model for behavior modification. Early counselors were carefully selected college students, and in recent years students have been joined by teachers highly trained in working with children who have special needs, so that the staff of counselors is balanced between those just gaining experience and those with years of experience behind them. Over the years, in the short span of a ten-day camp, the lives of hundreds of children have been turned around.

In the hymn for Englishton Park, I tried to capture the beauty of the setting, the strength of the program, and the loving quality of the people who live and work there.

2   When, in Awe of God's Creation

This hymn was written for the Presbyterian Peacemaking Program on its 1992 theme: "A World without Boundaries." The context is obviously the sight of our planet Earth from outer space. I have been moved by the comments of astronauts from *all* countries as they have seen our mutual home from afar, and as they have later reflected on that sight. One Christmas one of our children, knowing how I love the picture of Earth from "out there," gave me a poster, a photograph of the Earth with the simple words: "Love Your Mother." It was a perfect gift for me.

In the hymn, I try to express my delight in that sight and my sense that we *must* somehow learn to live together as citizens of the whole world, all children in the family of a loving Creator God. In a recent study of the book of Psalms, I was struck by the thought that this hymn is a modern echo of Psalm 8.

When I have used this hymn in worship or in workshops I have noticed how people respond, especially to the final stanza. While working on the text, I was not sure about those last four lines with the repeated command to "Love each other." The more I worked on it, the better it seemed as the hymn's conclusion—from question to possibility to affirmation to proclamation. The insistent repetition has moved some to tears. I suppose it is my current favorite of all my hymns.

I had ABBOT'S LEIGH in mind as I wrote the words, but that tune was less familiar than HYFRYDOL, which is also a favorite of mine. The hymn appeared with the latter tune when it first was included in a notebook of worship resources I compiled and edited for the Presbyterian Peacemaking Program (*Peacemaking through Worship*, vol. 2, produced in 1992). I have enjoyed the fact that HYFRYDFOL was written by Rowland Hugh Prichard when he was a teenager in 1831, and here it is coupled with words by a late-twentieth-century grandmother. *The Chalice Hymnal* of the Christian Church (Disciples of Christ), appearing in 1995, is the first denominational hymnal to have included this hymn. ABBOT'S LEIGH may be used as an alternate tune.

3   *Sovereign God of Every Creature*

In 1989 the Presbyterian Church (U.S.A.) was celebrating its bicentennial and launching the Bicentennial Fund, a major campaign to raise awareness and dollars for the mission of the church in all parts of the world. This hymn was written in recognition of the significance of that event and the fund.

HYMN TO JOY is a tune perhaps overused today, but I chose it hoping that the syncopated rhythm of Beethoven's Ninth Symphony, the origin of the melody, would be used. That requires a strong word at the beginning of the final "87" phrase, or between the third and fourth lines of the music as usually printed. I enjoyed achieving this with "Jar," "Teach," "Knit," and "Christ."

The call to stewardship of the whole creation and of all God's gifts entrusted to human care is the focus of this hymn. The importance of present action and decisiveness is also stressed. In the final stanza I like being able to use the phrase "Lead us not into temptation"; we repeat it so frequently in the Lord's Prayer that we slide right by it. This context may renew its meaning for some unsuspecting singer of hymns.

4   *Christ Has Come, Salvation Bringing!*

FABEN is a tune I had overlooked, and Easter is a celebration and a season about which I had not written a great deal previous to this hymn. The tune carries a sense of excitement and urgency that invites imperatives. So the text is full of exclamations and energy.

5   *O God of All Creation*

The theme of the 1991 Churchwide Gathering of Presbyterian Women was "Whose World Is It?" My sister-in-law, Joanne Lindberg Parker, chaired the program committee for the plenary sessions of the meeting, which were to be held in the sports arena of Iowa State University in Ames, Iowa, July 17–22, 1991. Early in 1990 I was asked to be the staff person for the program committee; it proved to be a challenging task, as dealing with ideas of theological, spiritual, and ecological depth hardly seemed to match the location of the meeting—a basketball coliseum.

The hymn deals primarily with God's sovereignty and creativity, but also with humanity's oneness with the rest of creation. It is not possible to deal honestly with our creatureliness without acknowledging how we fall short in our stewardship of creation and in our relationships, not only with other human beings, but with the rest of creation, and most of all, in our relationship to God.

Because there were to be a number of participants whose primary language was Spanish, this theme hymn was translated into Spanish and included in their Spanish Program Book. Yolanda Hernandez, Associate for the Women's Ministry Unit, asked our mutual friend Ana Inés Braulio to translate my words into Spanish to fit the music. It was not an easy task, and I am grateful for the time and care taken to accomplish it. The Spanish translation follows the original in English.

6   *O Dios de lo Creado*

See comment on no. 5, "O God of All Creation."

7   *We Sing Our Praise to God*

This hymn, written in 1990, was in response to the request from First Presbyterian Church in Decatur, Indiana, for a hymn to celebrate their sesquicentennial. When Dianne Linn, a member of the anniversary committee, called me, I asked for material about their church, as is my custom. Their first choice of tune was TERRA BEATA, so that is what I used. On receiving the hymn, Dianne wrote back:

> The hymn is perfect. It describes our church as I remember it from childhood and, more actively, as an adult. Our committee met last night, and everyone was very pleased.

It is a simple hymn of praise and thanksgiving, achieving one of my ongoing goals, to write hymns with only three stanzas. Not all hymns need to express one's complete theology or be lengthy! Nonetheless, gratitude and praise of God do indeed comprise a full expression of a joyful faith.

8 *Sing, My Soul, in Praise Unending*

This hymn was written for a conference theme, "Memory and Hope," to be held in the Presbytery of Blackhawk at their conference center, Stronghold. My friend Sue Shields was working on the conference, as was her husband, Dave, the executive presbyter. They requested a theme hymn. Other emphases were to be: stewardship, justice, love, peace, and reconciliation. The hymn becomes a joyful affirmation of hope because of God's activity in our lives.

At the same time, Sue was interested in a blessing to be sung before meals in the dining hall of Stronghold. It was to be written in letters large enough to be sung by the assembled people. Here is the verse I wrote, also to be sung to John Hughes's wonderful melody CWM RHONDDA.

> Thank You, God! Your love surrounds us
>   With provision for our need.
> In Your love, may we remember
>   Hungry ones whom we should feed.
>   Gracious God,
>   Abundant Giver,
>   Grant us strength to conquer greed.
>   Grant us grace to hear and heed!

9 *Planting Seeds of Faith and Trust*

The theme for the 1987 Youth Triennium for the Synod of Lincoln Trails was "Growing Together in Trust." I was asked to write a theme hymn, the stanzas of which would deal with the daily themes and biblical basis, as follows:

Daily Themes	Biblical Basis
1. Planting Seeds of Trust	Mark 4:26–29
	Luke 5:1–11

2.	Nurturing Trust	Mark 14:3–9
		Jer. 17:7–8
3.	Failing Trust	Isa. 40:6–8
		Mark 14:26–31, 66–72
4.	Blooming Trust	Mark 4:30–32
		John 21
5.	Scattering the Seeds of Trust	Matt. 28:16–20
		Mark 4:3–9

I thought it came out rather well!

10 *"God Is Love," the Bible Teaches*

The Hymnal Revision Committee of the General Conference of the United Methodist Church was interested in new hymns for children. This is a hymn I wrote to send to them, and although it did not make it into the *United Methodist Hymnal*, I still think it is a possible selection for children's voices. The repetition in the text makes for easy memorization, and the words are not too complex for youthful tongues.

The tune AR HYD Y NOS is one familiar, at least to older generations, in the lullaby "All Through the Night" ("Sleep, my child, and peace attend thee"). EAST ACKLAM is, I believe, the only other melody with this meter, having been written as a new tune for a text by Fred Pratt Green. Mr. Green's "For the Fruit of All Creation" was written with AR HYD Y NOS in mind, but the bolder EAST ACKLAM is better suited to his thanksgiving hymn.

11 *Gracious God of All Creation*

This hymn was written for the West Hollywood Presbyterian Church. In October 1989 I was in Los Angeles for a presbytery workshop on *The Presbyterian Hymnal: Hymns, Psalms, and Spiritual Songs,* which was due to come out the following year. The West Hollywood Church invited me to lead a hymn festival in their Sunday morning worship service the same weekend, and I accepted gladly.

The church is well known for its vigorous choir as well as for its ministry with the gay and lesbian community. The talented organist was determined to be there in spite of weakness due to his increasing struggle with AIDS. The music was tremendous! The hymn proved to be a strong affirmation of faith for all who were present.

The traditional Welsh tune AR HYD Y NOS, which many people first learned as a lullaby—"Sleep, my child, and peace attend thee, / All through the night"—was chosen for its comfort as well as its strength. The music lends itself to the repetition of the phrase "Your will be done"; and the longer meter halfway through provides for listing and emphasizing the messages included in the hymn.

12 *"I Am Who I Am, I Will Be Who I Will"*

13 *"I Am Who I Am"—Our Living God's Name*

These two hymns were inspired by the book *Reimagining God: The Case for Scriptural Diversity*, by Johanna W. H. van Wijk-Bos (Westminster John Knox Press, 1995). I realized that I had never seen a hymn using that mysterious phrase given by God to Moses in Exodus 3:13–14 and variously translated "I am who I am" or "I am what I am" or "I will be what I will be" or, as Johanna translates it, "I will be who I will be."

My first recollection of awareness of that phrase is from a 1942 required class in Bible at the Northfield School for Girls, now Northfield Mount Hermon School. I thought it was peculiar, but was intrigued enough with the turn of phrase that, four years later, I chose to take a year of Hebrew instead of Greek in fulfillment of a language requirement as a biblical history major at Wellesley. I have long since forgotten all Hebrew except for the first few words of Genesis and of the Shema, but I appreciate Johanna's marvelous unveiling of the language in her writing and teaching.

The major challenge was to find a metrical fit. Once into the project, I rather enjoyed being capricious with the combination of words and music, hoping that the surprising way the phrases move will contribute to the mystery of the "I will be who I will be!" I needed strong tunes to stand up to my mischief. ST DENIO and LYONS certainly fill the bill.

14 *Creator of Mountains*

"Creator of Mountains" was written for the installation of the Rev. Elizabeth Knott as executive of the Synod of Alaska-Northwest on October 25, 1987. That synod covers an area not only huge geographically, but diverse in cultures and rich in resources both human and physical. It was fun to put these words together. There are some unusual images of God—how often have we thought of God as a "Splasher of fountains"? The internal rhyming in the middle of the last two lines of each stanza appeals to my love of rhyme. Being a devotee of meter, I also particularly like "faith, like a drumbeat, keeps steady our praise."

The tune, ST. DENIO, in some hymnals is named JOANNA. In any case, it is a strong Welsh melody most often associated with "Immortal, Invisible, God Only Wise."

15 *Word of God in Human Language*

Not long before the publication of the New Revised Standard Version of the Bible (NRSV) , I happened to be at a conference with Eileen Lindner, who was then working for the National Council of Churches (NCC). She mentioned that worship materials were being prepared to assist in the introduction of the NRSV to the church and the world, and she wondered if I might be interested in writing a hymn for inclusion in the materials.

I wrote three hymns for that purpose in 1989: "All Praise to God for Word and Words," "God of All Communication," and this one.

There is some repetition among them, but each one stands in its own right, focusing on a different aspect of what it means to have the "Word of God in human language / For this time and in our tongue." There is some advantage in having a choice between a short hymn or a longer one, and the particular tune that is chosen contributes to the sense of the words.

For all the hymns, I suggested several possibilities for tunes. The one chosen by the NCC for reproduction in the promotional materials is printed here with these words. The other suggested tunes are listed in the notes about each hymn for information, and to illustrate how the choice of tune can influence the mood and the power of the words. The alternate tune suggested for "Word of God in Human Language" is ABBOT'S LEIGH. Wisely, in each case the people at the National Council chose a tune in public domain, thus avoiding copyright problems with reprintings.

Of the three hymns, this one is the strongest call to action in response to receiving the Word. It also speaks of spiritual hunger for the message.

16 *God of All Communication*

This is one of three hymns written for the introduction of the New Revised Standard Version of the Bible (NRSV) in 1989. "All Praise to God for Word and Words" and "Word of God in Human Language" are the others; for background on the three, see individual comments and especially those for "Word of God in Human Language."

Those responsible for designing worship materials for the NRSV introduction chose the tune HYMN TO JOY for its joyfulness and familiarity. BLAEN-HAFREN is printed here because I love Welsh melodies and to illustrate the interaction of words and music.

An intriguing exercise I have sometimes used in workshops is to have the group sing each stanza of this hymn to a different tune, beginning with HYMN TO JOY and moving down the following list. Not being a pianist, I need and appreciate great help from the musician at the keyboard!

Alternate tunes are HYMN TO JOY (Ludwig van Beethoven, 1824), BLAEN-HAFREN (Welsh melody), IN BABILONE (Dutch melody), EBENEZER (Thomas John Williams, 1890).

Joy, thoughtfulness, solemnity, movement, power—these are some of the factors quite noticeable as one or another of the suggested tunes is used.

The hymn is full of references to those who have contributed to our having the Bible in our time and in our language: prophets, martyrs, storytellers, historians, priests, singers, scholars, translators, and above all Christ, the Living Word.

17 *Words Are Tools of Peace and Justice*

This hymn was written for an emphasis of the National Council of Churches on inclusive language as a justice issue. It was the first of several hymns dealing with the importance of the words we use in our language with and about people, and in our language about God.

I like words! I appreciate the beauty of expression possible in the English language, and I know that it is *not* true that "Sticks and stones may break my bones, / but words will never hurt me!" Words can indeed hurt. They can also heal.

18 *All Praise to God for Word and Words*

This is one of three hymns written for the introduction of the New Revised Standard Version of the Bible (NRSV) in 1989. It is a simple hymn of grateful praise, noting the gratitude all readers should feel for those who have preserved the words and manuscripts over the centuries. I particularly like the use of the word "illuminating" in the second stanza, evoking the elaborately artistic illuminated manuscripts of the centuries before the printing press was invented. The hymn is also a reminder that the Word needs to be *heard* (not necessarily with ears, but with the heart), and its message is to be *received* and *lived*.

Several tunes in both Common Meter (CM) and Common Meter Double (CMD) were suggested for possible use with this text.

Alternate tunes in Common Meter are EVAN (William Henry Havergal, 1846), DALEHURST (Arthur Cottman, 1874), and AMAZING GRACE (*Virginia Harmony*, 1831; arr. Edwin O. Excell, 1900).

Alternate tunes in Common Meter Double are FOREST GREEN (English folk melody, arr. Ralph Vaughan Williams, 1906) and ELLACOMBE (*Gesangbuch der Herzogl. Wirtembergischen Katholischen Hofkapelle*, 1784, alt. 1868).

If CMD is used, as in ELLACOMBE or FOREST GREEN, it becomes a hymn with just two stanzas, combining the first two into one, and the last two into the second. Those preparing the materials for introducing the NRSV wisely chose ST. ANNE, since it is a strong tune, very familiar and in public domain.

19 *We Will Sing a Song of Women*

This is more like a "fun song" than a hymn. One clue is that it is a challenge to fit the words to the notes, since they come apace! I wrote this in 1989 in fulfillment of a commission from Judson Press for a hymn about women in the Bible. The second stanza ("Sarah, Hagar, Leah . . .") was added in 1995 when we were going to sing the hymn at a Spring Gathering of Presbyterian Women in the Presbytery of Ohio Valley. The theme of the meeting was "Listening to Our Sisters," with the focus on women whom we too often overlook. Certainly some of the women of the Bible who are mentioned here fit that category.

I like the bit of mischief in using a tune named ARMAGEDDON!

20 *The Lord's My Shepherd*

This paraphrase of Psalm 23 was written for consideration by the committee preparing *The Presbyterian Hymnal: Hymns, Psalms, and Spiritual Songs* (Westminster/John Knox Press, 1990). I was serving on the committee and on its subcommittee working on the extensive psalm section of the hymnal. We had available several traditional settings of the Twenty-third Psalm and several tunes associated with the texts. We wanted to include some traditional texts and some in more contemporary language. DOMINUS REGIT ME was a tune the committee wished to use, but it needed a new set of words using inclusive language. I wrote these words for them to consider in my absence, that being the practice for work submitted by members of the hymnal committee. It was accepted for publication in the *Hymnal*.

I particularly like some of the phrases that are more nearly the way believers today would say them, such as: "My cup is full, and more than full . . . ," which sounds generous but not wasteful.

21 *Your Word, O God, a Sharpened Blade*

I had been working on making language more inclusive for several years, still learning implications, still gaining new insights and sensitivities, when the National Council announced a conference on "Language and Justice" to be held at the Stony Point Conference Center, Stony Point, New York, June 26–30, 1987. This hymn about the power of words and the one immediately above were written for that conference. A few years later, with the introduction of the New Revised Standard Version of the Bible (NRSV), I had another opportunity to write about the importance of words.

22 *God of Time and Space and Thought*

Pioneers of Faith
Remembering the 1853–54 Whitworth wagon train:
westward to Olympia, Washington

"God of Time and Space and Thought" was written at the request of

David Webster, the brother of Dan Webster, who sings in the same church choir I do. David, a member of Westminster Presbyterian Church in Olympia, Washington, was interested in celebrating the anniversary of the Whitworth wagon train, 1853–54, along the Oregon Trail. The westward movement of Presbyterians was significant for my McAfee forebears at the beginning of the Oregon Trail on the border between Missouri and Kansas, and for the Websters' at the northwestern end of the Trail.

When I asked for a suggestion of a tune, David Webster resurrected the tune AMSTERDAM, which had been unknown to me. The tune marvelously evokes the plodding, difficult journey of pioneer settlers who moved westward, compelled to share the good news as they understood it. I especially like the interruption of the regularity of the meter in the third phrase; it seems to force us to keep going on when the inclination would be to ease back into a more comfortable pattern. The irregular meter means that the hymn does not fit any other tune so far as I know, but I enjoyed the fact that the unusual metrical pattern presented a particular challenge in "getting it right."

There is a trinitarian motif in the stanzas of this hymn honoring the "Pioneers of Faith," who followed their call enduring hardship and separation from loved ones for the sake of their God.

23 We Remember with Thanksgiving

In 1986 the Presbyterian Church (U.S.A.) was celebrating 150 years of the denomination's participation in ecumenical mission. This hymn, written for that celebration, is a fairly straightforward one about the past, present, and future of ecumenical relationships and ecumenical mission. The first stanza honors pioneer workers in this field whose motivation was to be faithful to Jesus' prayer "that they may all be one." The second stanza alludes to the great variety of cooperative work: institutions of learning, hospitals and medical schools, writing and translating, in addition to evangelism. The third stanza calls for a renewed commitment to Christ's mission appropriate for this and future times.

The tune NETTLETON was chosen as one that would have been known and sung at the time of the nineteenth-century missionary movement that spread the gospel with such energy into all the world.

24 God Is Here in Word and Action

The Madison Presbyterian Church in Madison, Indiana, was planning a celebration of its Korean connections, to take place on Sunday, October 3, 1993, World Communion Sunday. The Moffett family, who for two generations served in Korea, came originally from Madison and called that church their

home church in this country. For the weekend of celebration, Howard and
Delle Moffett were to be present along with others in the family. The Korean
Presbyterian Church of Cincinnati, seventy-five miles up the Ohio River, had
been in touch with the Madison church because of the Moffett connection,
and they too were to be part of the celebration.

The request came to me through Marie Cross, the pastor in Madison at
the time, for a hymn that celebrated global mission and world connections
and that spoke of the more recent ways we "do mission" together as
partners. I wrote two hymns for them to consider: "O God in Christ, You
Call Us into Mission" and this one, "God Is Here in Word and Action." This
was their choice for the celebration, perhaps because it begins with the
strong affirmation that God is present everywhere, even before we come
upon the scene, geographically or chronologically!

Theresa Bauer, the director of music at the Madison church, tried the
words with every hymn tune in 87 87 D meter in the recently published
Presbyterian Hymnal: Hymns, Psalms, and Spiritual Songs. C. Hubert H.
Parry's RUSTINGTON was her excellent choice.

25 *O God in Christ, You Call Us into Mission*

This is one of two hymns I sent to Marie Cross, who was pastor of
Madison Presbyterian Church in Madison, Indiana, when that church was
planning a celebration of its connection with mission in Korea, especially
through the Moffetts, who spent many years there. The celebration was to
take place on the first Sunday in October 1993, World Communion Sunday.
The committee chose to use the other hymn, "God Is Here in Word and
Action," set to the tune RUSTINGTON. This hymn is slower and more contemp-
lative no matter what tune of this meter one uses. I chose CONSOLATION,
although CHARTERHOUSE or WELWYN work well too. The emphasis in the high
note of the third line of CONSOLATION suits the text nicely: "Challenged to
love," "May we, like *them*," and "Make clear the *call*."

26 *Loving God of All Creation*

My friend Marie Cross, pastor of the Madison Presbyterian Church in
Madison, Indiana, at the time, asked if I would write a hymn celebrating the
global witness and mission of the church. The congregation was planning a
celebration of the global missionary movement and its connections with
the local church. Marie was particularly interested in expressing some of
the ways in which the Presbyterian Church (U.S.A.) carries out its global
witness and mission today. Some of the hymns written in the height of
the missionary fervor of the latter half of the nineteenth century have a
triumphal tone, an almost (if not actual) militant urgency to *conquer* for
Christ. Today, by contrast, missionaries are invited by the church in another

country to fill a specific need, and missionaries come at our invitation to help us see the whole church in a new light.

27 *Holy God of All Creation*

In 1991 the National Council of the Churches of Christ in the U.S.A. was introducing a series of consultations across the United States dealing with the serious societal problems facing the nation, the world, and the church. The consultations were titled: "Toward a World Made New"—launching "The New World Order Project: Christian Visions of a World Made New."

This hymn was written for those consultations. Its references to homelessness, pollution, urban unrest, and runaway and otherwise lost children are current concerns in our time. These are added to the perennial problems of the human condition: war and natural disasters. But we know, as followers of Christ, that hope and promise and visions of a world made new are the ultimate response.

Will the problems ever be solved so that these words become obsolete? I hope so.

28 *Holy God, We Name You*

With Presbyterian reunion in 1983 came a decision to relocate the denominational offices, with the result that within a few years many staff persons moved from New York City and Atlanta to Louisville, Kentucky. Among these were a number who had been active in Central Presbyterian Church in downtown Atlanta, just across the street from the state capitol. Several had also been members of the choir, and two of these persons approached me about writing a hymn to be a gift to Central Presbyterian Church from grateful former members.

Not understanding their full intent, I first wrote a rather innocuous song of praise about singing in a choir. It was *not* what they had in mind. We arranged a luncheon get-together in the midst of a General Assembly Council meeting, at which about a dozen former members of Central sat around the table with me reminiscing and talking about the impact of that congregation and its ministry and mission on their lives. They also especially asked if the tune KING'S WESTON could be used. "Holy God, We Name You" is the result—much stronger and more to their liking!

29 *Seeking to Be Faithful Servants*

Early in 1989 I had a request for a hymn to address the theme of the Global Mission Conference of the Presbyterian Church (U.S.A.) to be held at Montreat Conference Center in North Carolina in July. "Mission in Christ's Way" was the theme I was given, along with a list of subthemes:

Turning to the Living God; Participation in Suffering and Struggle; The Earth Is the Lord's; and Renewed Communities in Mission. As a rule, I think hymns should have fewer than five stanzas, and I do not often repeat stanza 1 as the last stanza; but it somehow seemed appropriate to do so here for emphasis, for dealing fully with the theme and subthemes, and for completion of the text. I like the recurring "one in Christ and one with neighbor."

30 *Loving Spirit, Our Creator*

This hymn, with much the same text as no. 33, was written for a meter of 87 87 87, one "87" phrase shorter than that hymn. It calls for a different rhyme scheme (ABCBDB—God, sod, trod) instead of the simpler (ABCB plus DEFE—God, sod; call, all). Both hymns are included here as an illustration of the intricacies, delights, and challenges of writing in meter.

31 *Christ, You Give Us Living Water*

Presbyterian Men were preparing for their 1991 Assembly when they requested a hymn to highlight their theme and their support of water projects in various parts of the world. It seemed to be an opportunity to call attention to several significant biblical references to water:

"living water," the Samaritan woman at the well	John 4
Jesus' washing his disciples' feet	John 13
baptism (of Jesus)	Matt. 3; Mark 1; Luke 3
baptism (of believers and households)	Matt. 28, Mark 16, Acts, many epistles

The third stanza points to the other sacrament observed by Presbyterians, and the new life offered to believers in the two sacraments of Baptism and the Lord's Supper.

The fourth stanza calls us, as followers of Christ, to be in ministry and mission in the world.

When I sent the hymn, I suggested three possible tunes: EBENEZER, by Thomas John Williams, 1890; FABEN, by John H. Willcox, 1849; and AUSTRIAN HYMN, by Franz Joseph Haydn, which is the one they chose.

32 *Gratefully Offer Talents and Service*

With Presbyterian reunion accomplished in 1983, the women's programs of the two uniting denominations worked together in a joint committee to design a new reality for women in the reunited church. The groups with the longest tradition of "women's work" extending into local associations became Presbyterian Women (PW). Facilitators of the work of "PW" were to be called PW Enablers. This short hymn was written for the first training meeting for this cadre of women, chosen to initiate the program of assistance to local groups.

The folk tune BUNESSAN suits the joy and energy of the words and of the program for which the text was written.

33 *Loving Spirit, Great Creator*

In July 1992, Carolyn Dick of American Baptist Women's Ministries (ABWM) asked if I would write a hymn for the launching of ABWM's "new day" the next year. They wanted a hymn to reflect their new mission statement, which states:

> In commitment to Jesus Christ as Lord and Savior,
>   and to the mission of the church,
>   and through the enabling of the Holy Spirit,
> AMERICAN BAPTIST WOMEN'S MINISTRIES
>   provides opportunities for each woman to:
>   become and develop as God's person,
>   build God's faith community, and
>   serve God's world.

The focus was to be on personal development, church and community, and mission and service.

When I sent the draft of the hymn, I noted that it was longer than I would prefer, but I wanted to use the three elements of their focus, and some sort of beginning and ending seemed necessary. I also pointed out that, in the next to last stanza, the phrase "Women working" could be changed to "People working" (as printed here) for more general use, but considering the ABWM context, this seemed appropriate for the launching of their "new day."

In addition to HYFRYDOL, Beethoven's HYMN TO JOY and the Dutch melody IN BABILONE were suggested as alternate tunes. (See comment on no. 30.)

34 *Sovereign God of All Creation*

This hymn I found buried in a folder labeled "In Process." It is trinitarian without using the traditional formula, and without discussing the internal relationships of the persons of the Trinity. In my opinion, the interrelationships are best expressed in shared concerns and mutually supportive actions. That is what I hoped to convey in these words.

35 *God beyond Us, God within Us*

A telephone call and letter from Ruth McCreath in the Office of the

General Assembly Council asked me to write a hymn for use with a "Vision for the Presbyterian Church (U.S.A.)," which a committee had been asked to prepare in connection with Churchwide Mission Goals for 1991–99. After receiving some background and notes from Ruth, I sent a draft for her to present to the committee. At their request I met with them, talked over some of their suggestions, did some rewriting, and this hymn was acceptable to all concerned.

The committee chose the tune HYMN TO JOY for its energy and joyfulness. In submitting the rewritten hymn, I wrote to Ruth:

> You will see that I altered each stanza slightly to put a "word-worth-emphasizing" at the beginning of the second to last line (Called, Christ, Teach, Giving). There is something to be said for using the "new" (that is, *original*) rhythm as it appears in *The Presbyterian Hymnal* [the rhythm chosen]; but there is also something to be said for using the "good old familiar" rhythm.

36 *Sing We Now of Peace with Justice*

This hymn for World Communion Sunday, 1989, was written for the Presbyterian Peacemaking Program. In the Presbyterian Church (U.S.A.), peacemaking is in particular focus each year on World Communion Sunday, the first Sunday in October; hence the final stanza of this hymn speaks of the healing that comes in the sacrament. The hymn also deals with human problems of hunger, disease, war, and violence, present realities even when we come to the Lord's Supper.

In 1989 American Baptist Women asked me to write a hymn for their activities and observance of the "Ecumenical Decade: Churches in Solidarity with Women." I used this same tune and the repeated "Peace with justice!" I think that hymn, "Praise the God Who Formed and Loved Us," has been more widely used than this one.

37 *"Peace to You"—These Words of Jesus*

I am grateful to Rich Killmer of the Presbyterian Peacemaking Program, who keeps asking for new hymns related to peacemaking. His prodding keeps me focused on the issues surrounding peacemaking in our time, and helps stretch the implications of our calling as peacemakers to new levels. In December 1994 he called about a hymn for the Presbyterian Peacemaking Program 1995. This text is the result. I suggested several possible tunes other than HYFRYDOL, which we have used before. My first choice would have been ABBOT'S LEIGH (Cyril Vincent Taylor, 1941), but it is still not very familiar to Presbyterians in spite of its appearance four times in *The Presbyterian Hymnal* of 1990. So I wrote to Rich:

GENEVA (George Henry Day, 1940) would also work with the words, but it is a little busier. . . . The other two are in public domain. IN BABILONE [the tune chosen] is more familiar, but it is a little bouncy for the words. RUSTINGTON (C. Hubert H. Parry, 1897) is not actually new, though fairly new to Presbyterians. It's in the hymnal three times!

I noted some Biblical references for your information, not expecting them to be printed with the hymn.

The biblical references are included here for the reader's interest:

"Peace to you"—these words of Jesus   *John 20:19*
Raise our hopes for peace on earth.
Peace!—the message sung by angels   *Luke 2:14*
Heralding our Savior's birth.
Peace!—the resurrection greeting!   *John 20:19*
Peace!—dispelling doubt and fear.
Peace!—the world's long-cherished vision,
Peace for all, both far and near.   *Eph. 2:14*

Peace will never be discovered   *Jer. 6:10–14*
While the hungry go unfed.
Peace remains a dim illusion
Till each child has home and bed.
If our systems crush the spirit,
Seeds of enmity are sown.
If we only think of winning,
Peace and justice are unknown.

Roads to peace are often rocky,
Challenging our very soul.
"Christ, our Peace" must be our watchword;   *Eph. 2:14*
Christ, the pathway; Christ, the goal.
Whether inner conflict rages,
Or relationships are torn
In our nations or our households,
Love, through Christ, can be reborn.

"Peace to you!"—A call to action,   *John 20:19*
Not a sentimental phrase;
Peace erasing every barrier,
Undergirding all our ways.
"Peace," Christ's resurrection greeting,
Still dispels our doubt and fright,
Building unity of spirit—
Christ, our Peace, our Hope, our Light.   *Eph. 2:14*

38 *Justice Is a Journey Onward*

The request for a hymn to be used in the twenty-fifth-anniversary celebration of the Self-Development of People (SDOP) in April 1995 came to me in the fall of 1994.

The SDOP Mission Statement says:

> Self-Development of People is a ministry which affirms God's concern for humankind. We are Presbyterian and non-Presbyterian people, dissatisfied with poverty and oppression, united in faith and action through sharing, confronting, and enabling. We participate in the empowerment of poor, oppressed and disadvantaged people seeking to change the structures that perpetuate poverty, oppression and injustice.

For many years I had been aware of SDOP as an outstanding example of a new way to deal with human problems, by assisting people in their projects through grants or loans to groups seeking to become self-supporting and independent. I had available a copy of the report of the special task force (1993) to evaluate the program. That report is titled "A Journey to Justice," and that seemed to me to be an appropriate focus for this hymn.

For strong words about justice, a strong tune was needed. I suggested several. EBENEZER, with its triplets and minor key, provides the desired emphasis and "seriousness." RUSTINGTON was another possibility, but is less familiar. The committee chose Haydn's AUSTRIAN HYMN for its strength and familiarity.

Following the celebration Fredric Walls, director of SDOP, wrote:

> I want to add my thanks and those of the National Committee on the Self-Development of People for the excellent and meaningful hymn you wrote for the 25th Anniversary of the unique Self-Development ministry. The hymn was sung joyfully throughout the Convocation. When we closed the event with your hymn, it was a moving moment and a fitting conclusion to the celebration.

What a delight to have been part of it!

39 *O Give God the Praise for Friendships That Last*

The Council on Women and the Church (COWAC) of the United Presbyterian Church U.S.A. and the Committee on Women's Concerns (COWC) of the Presbyterian Church U.S. had been working together for several years to be part of their denominational reunion into the Presbyterian Church (U.S.A.). Their final meeting before becoming a new creation in the new church's structure was a celebration of work done and work still ahead. This hymn, perhaps more appropriately a song, was sung as part of that celebration.

Originally the tune was LYONS, but since that tune appears elsewhere in this collection and HANOVER does not, I decided to present it here with the latter tune. I am rightly accused of bias in favor of HANOVER, even though the tune came long before the existence of my favorite hometown and college!

40 *O God of Earth and Altar*

The alterations to the text of "O God of Earth and Altar" were requested by Dr. Lewis Mudge, then dean of McCormick Theological Seminary in Chicago. Dr. Mudge was one of the theologians assisting in the writing of a "Life and Mission Statement" for the recently reunited Presbyterian Church (U.S.A.) at a consultation held at Mo Ranch, Texas, in mid-February 1985. The leaders wanted to use the hymn during the closing worship service at the consultation. They appreciated the strong tune and text, but thought some of the language (e.g., "prince and priest and thrall") was not as meaningful in the present context as it had been when written by a resident of the British Isles. In addition, the text was written in 1906, long before issues of inclusive language were raised and when the usual form for addressing God was in the second person singular ("Thee, Thy," etc.).

It was the last evening of the consultation when Dr. Mudge asked what could be done about the text. Attempting to keep the force and clarity of Chesterton's text and to incorporate contemporary concerns about the church's mission in the world, in the second stanza "lies of tongue and pen" became "lies of pen and voice" that "make our hearts rejoice" instead of "comfort cruel men." The third stanza puts the *ideas* of the original author in contemporary language: unity and action for peace and justice under God's guidance and direction.

The alterations were completed in less than a couple of hours during the evening and were presented to the worship leaders early the following morning, just in time for the worship service for which they were intended. The service was the closing event of the Consultation on the Life and Mission Statement for the Presbyterian Church (U.S.A.), February 17, 1985.

41 *Praise the God Who Formed and Loved Us*

A request from American Baptist Women's Ministries in 1989 for a hymn celebrating the "Ecumenical Decade: Churches in Solidarity with Women" led to the writing of this hymn using as a refrain the phrase "Peace with justice." The previous year I had written a hymn for World Communion Sunday, 1989, for the Presbyterian Peacemaking Program. "Sing We Now of Peace with Justice" (see no. 36) is set to the same tune and also uses "Peace with justice" as its refrain. I like the strength and imperative of such a phrase where we have habitually sung "Alleluia!"

Each hymn has its own merit. This one for ABWM highlights issues related to women that face the churches today: vocation and societal problems, especially as they impact the lives of women and children.

42 *God of Our Years*

This was the first text I sent to The Ladue Chapel, in St. Louis, Missouri, in response to their request for a hymn celebrating their fiftieth anniversary. Their music and arts committee, through the associate pastor, W. Clarence Koon, Jr. ("Dub"), asked for more emphasis on God's action in the future, especially as God is "in our lives leading the way rather than filling us with new inspiration." I went back to square one, and "God of Days and Years and Eons" (no. 44) was the result.

43 *God of Life, in Christ You Lead Us*

Helen Wright, of Coshocton, Ohio, called me in the fall of 1992, asking if I would write a hymn for the 175th anniversary of the Presbyterian church there. Following our telephone conversation, in a letter dated October 23, she outlined their plans this way:

> We want a hymn that is general in nature, which can be used by the whole church for anniversaries as well as other occasions. However, we want it to reflect our theme, which is "Celebrating our Past, Consecrating our Future."

> We would like for you to use the tune Abbot's Leigh.

Enclosed with the letter were a history of the church, some present interests and concerns of the congregation, and several copies of the church newsletter, *The Carillon.* I was to complete the hymn by Christmas in order that a festival setting could be composed for a premier presentation on March 24, 1993. Given these rich resources, the hymn came to life rather quickly. On November 4, 1992, I wrote to Helen:

> As you can see, sometimes the "Muse of Hymnody" works more quickly than at other times! The enclosed four stanzas came fairly easily. After letting them jell for a while and doing some reworking, I decided to send them along for you to ponder. I am always glad when I can send a hymn early enough so that if there are any needed changes, there is time to work on them.

> Please be assured that I am open to your comments. As you will note, the final two lines required the addition of the "present" to

your anniversary theme; and they will be easier to sing when inter-
lined with the music, since the first syllable of each of the last two
lines needs the two notes tied as in the music.

One valid test of a new text is whether *other* people can sing it! You
may want to try it with your choir.

The pastor, church musicians, and the committee approved the draft,
and here is the hymn.

44 God of Days and Years and Eons

This hymn was written for the fiftieth anniversary of The Ladue Chapel,
Presbyterian Church (U.S.A.), in St. Louis, Missouri. The request had come
through W. Clarence Koon, Jr. ("Dub"), an associate pastor at the church. The
first hymn I sent for their consideration was set to the tune LOBE DEN HERREN
(no. 42), and, as is my practice, I invited their suggestions, offering to try a
"good old 87 87 D" if this draft did not seem right for them. The response was
to request a text set to HYMN TO JOY (87 87 D), and that is what I gave them.

45 O Faithful God of Years Long Past

In November 1988, Dennis Elwell, music director and organist at the
Overbrook Presbyterian Church in Philadelphia, wrote to inquire about my
writing a hymn for Overbrook's centennial celebration to be held on
Sunday, October 29, 1989. He wrote:

> Specifically, the committee has chosen the hymn tune WEYMOUTH, by
> Theodore P. Ferris (1941), for which they would like a text. Though
> WEYMOUTH does not appear in the Presbyterian hymnbooks, it can
> be found in the Episcopal *Hymnal 1940* at number 401. It is a
> beautiful, singable, and very easily learned tune in Common Metre
> Double. You may well be familiar with it.

Although I did not know the tune, I found it singable (as promised) and
easy to use. When I sent a draft, the committee made several good suggestions
for alteration. The resulting text, commissioned as part of the Barnard
Commissions for the Centennial of Overbrook, proved to be satisfactory for
all concerned.

46 God of Beginnings

Here is a hymn about partnership on the journey, whether it is life's
journey, an institution's journey, a denomination's journey, or the whole
church's journey.

CRUSADERS' HYMN has such a distinctive meter that it is unlikely that any
text would fit except for one written specifically for this tune. Working with

a hymn named for the Crusaders brought to mind that era and what seem today to have been the errors in judgment that led to the slaughter of so many people on all sides in the conflict. I like the fact of claiming the mystery of God and confessing our history so that we can move on into whatever lies ahead, confident of God's continuing presence in the person of Jesus Christ.

47 *O God, You Call to Service Day by Day*

The request for a new hymn for the installation of a pastor in First Presbyterian Church, Allentown, Pennsylvania, came to me from Gloria S. Snyder, director of music. Anticipating the arrival of the new pastor, Jefferson K. Aiken, she wrote:

> Our theme for this spring has been, "As We Move Forward." The promise of the arrival of our new pastor is a major milestone for our congregation, one that we expect will fill us with a new burst of creative energy, refreshing us all with a clearer vision of our ministry. This is truly an exciting time for us.

Following the installation service in September 1992, she sent a copy of the bulletin for the occasion and wrote:

> Our installation service . . . was powerful and exciting beyond describing. And our new hymn played a large role in the creation of that atmosphere. . . . From my vantage point in the Choir Loft, I could enjoy the positive facial expressions of many of our Session members. In particular, the reaction of our stewardship leaders, as we returned to your thought-provoking use of the phrase "As we move forward," was absolutely thrilling.

It is a delight when the muse of creativity matches words to expectations!

48 *O Gracious God, by Whom the Church Is Founded*

First Presbyterian Church of Morgantown, West Virginia, was planning its bicentennial celebration in 1988. I had met the pastor, Richard Fiete, since we were both on denominational committees at the time. When he asked me about writing a hymn for their anniversary, I replied (as I usually do) that I would like to have some materials in order to learn more about the church—its history, its mission, its characteristics, its emphases, its hopes. There is a genuine satisfaction in trying to match words with a congregation and thereby meeting their expectations.

I had asked about possible tunes they might like to use. The choice of WELWYN offers longer phrases and a smoother line than in the more standard meters, although the average singer may need to breathe more often than the punctuation suggests!

49 *Creator God, You Build Your Church*

Five years after reunion of the Presbyterian churches that had been separated since the Civil War, the "new" Presbyterian Church (U.S.A.) was ready to move into a newly restored building, the Presbyterian Center in Louisville, Kentucky. This hymn was written for the dedication of that center in October 1988. It was sung by the assembled crowd grouped around the northern face of the building on a bright and brisk autumn day. Although written for a denominational building, it would be appropriate for the dedication of any church structure.

50 *Open the Doors for Christ!*

This hymn was written for the dedication of a new worship building for Overlake Park Presbyterian Church in Bellevue, Washington. The theme for the move into the new facility was "Open the Doors." David R. Wright, the pastor, wrote:

> Our campus is made up of five different buildings, and the worship building is one of those. In April of 1987 there was a fire that very quickly destroyed the building. On the Sunday following the fire we gathered in front of the building and had a service where we closed the doors for the final time and then moved to our Fellowship Hall, where we have been worshiping for the last two years. We used the theme "Open the Doors" for the financial campaign for the new building. And now I envision a service of dedication, a part of that being opening the doors to go into the new worship building.

The congregation had suffered four years of sadness: the sudden death of a parish associate, departures, disappointments, and disease. All this in addition to the fire.

Imagine my surprise when I read some of the early history of the congregation and discovered that my younger sister and her family had been charter members of Overlake Park Presbyterian Church when it was organized in 1959!

It was a pleasure to be part of their rebuilding and movement into a new era of worship and service.

51 *O God, You Build the Church*

The Hitchcock Presbyterian Church in Scarsdale, New York, to which my friend Kathy Lancaster had belonged, suffered a terribly destructive fire. As the congregation undertook the task of rebuilding, Kathy and Lew Lancaster wanted to give them a lasting gift and asked if I might write a hymn for the church to use when the newly restored building was to be dedicated.

Although this hymn was written for a congregation's rebuilding after a devastating fire, I think it speaks to the "building up of the church" in other ways as well.

LEONI is a great tune, and it suits the solemnity and hope I tried to convey in the words.

52 *Rejoice! Our Loving God*

This simple hymn of praise was written during the celebration of the bicentennial of the Presbyterian Church in this country. Its stanzas celebrate past, present, and future. The words honor God's reign and realm while acknowledging the constant need for the reforming power and love of Christ. I make no apologies for the continuation of the refrain traditionally associated with the tune MARION.

Index of Churches, Programs, and Individuals for Whom the Hymns Were Written

American Baptist Women's Ministries, 33, 41

Bicentennial Fund Campaign, Presbyterian Church (U.S.A.), 3

Central Presbyterian Church, Atlanta, Georgia, 28

Committee for a New Presbyterian Hymnal, Presbyterian Church (U.S.A.), 20

Committee on Women's Concerns, Presbyterian Church U.S., 39

Coshocton Presbyterian Church, Coshocton, Ohio, 43

Council on Women and the Church, United Presbyterian Church U.S.A., 39

Cross, Marie, 24–26

Elwell, Dennis, 45

Englishton Park Presbyterian Ministries, Inc., Lexington, Indiana, 1

Fiete, Richard, 48

First Presbyterian Church, Allentown, Pennsylvania, 47

First Presbyterian Church, Decatur, Indiana, 7

First Presbyterian Church, Morgantown, West Virginia, 48

Global Mission Conference, 29

Hitchcock Presbyterian Church, Scarsdale, New York, 51

Knott, Elizabeth, 14

Ladue Chapel Presbyterian Church, St. Louis, Missouri, 42, 44

Lancaster, Kathy, 51

Linn, Dianne, 7

Madison Presbyterian Church, Madison, Indiana, 24–26

National Council of the Churches of Christ in the U.S.A., 15–18, 21, 27

New Revised Standard Version of the Bible (NRSV), 15, 16, 18

Overbrook Presbyterian Church, Philadelphia, Pennsylvania, 45

Overlake Park Presbyterian Church, Bellevue, Washington, 50

Presbyterian Church U.S., 39

Presbyterian Church (U.S.A.), 3, 20, 23, 29, 35, 40, 49

Presbyterian Men, Presbyterian Church (U.S.A.), 31

Presbyterian Peacemaking Program, Presbyterian Church (U.S.A.), 2, 36, 37

Presbyterian Women, Presbyterian Church (U.S.A.), 5, 6, 32

Presbyterian Women in the Presbytery of Ohio Valley, 19

Presbytery of Blackhawk, Stronghold Conference Center, 8

Presbytery of Ohio Valley, Presbyterian Women, 19

Self Development of People, Presbyterian Church (U.S.A.), 38

Shields, Sue and David, 8

Snyder, Gloria S., 47

Stronghold Conference Center, Presbytery of Blackhawk, 8

Synod of Alaska-Northwest, 14

Synod of Lincoln Trails, Youth Triennium, 9

United Methodist Hymnal Committee, 10

United Presbyterian Church U.S.A., 39

Webster, David, 22

West Hollywood Presbyterian Church, West Hollywood, California, 11

Westminster Presbyterian Church, Olympia, Washington, 22

Wright, David R., 50

Wright, Helen, 43

Index of Scriptural Allusions

Genesis

1	2, 3, 5–7, 14, 27
7—9	13
9:12–17	35
12—23	19

Exodus

1:15–20	19
2:21–22	19
3:13–14	12, 13
14	13

Deuteronomy

32:11	12

Judges

4—5	19

Ruth 19

1 Samuel

1	19

Esther 19

Psalms

8	2
18; 19	12
31; 62	12
23	20

Isaiah

11	27
40:8	15, 16, 18
40:31	39
42:10–12	14

Isaiah (continued)

44:9–20	13
45:18–21	2, 13

Jeremiah

6:10–14	37
17:7–8	9

Ezekiel

37	13

Amos

7	13

Micah

6:8	8, 38, 40

Malachi

3:2	51

Matthew

1:23	12
3:16	12, 31
6:10	11
8:23–27	13
10:7	52
13:1–23	9
25:31–46	3
26:26–30	31
28:1–10	4, 19, 24
28:16–20	9, 22–25, 27

Mark

1:10	12, 31
4:1–29	9
4:35–41	13

Mark (continued)

14:22–25	31
16	4, 19, 24

Luke

2:14	37
3:22	12, 31
5:1–11	9
6:13–16	9
8:4–15	9
8:22–25	13
10:9–11	52
11:1–4	11
17:21	52
22:14–21	31
24:1–12	4, 19, 24

John

1	15, 16, 18
1:32	12, 31
4	31
11	13
13	26, 31, 34
14:6	22
17:23	36, 41, 47
20:1–18	4, 19, 24
20:19	37
21:15–17	15, 27

Acts

2	4, 12, 13, 50
16	19
18	19

Romans

16	19

1 Corinthians

1:30	12

Galatians

6:2	38

Ephesians

2:14	37
2:20	3

Colossians

1:15–20	4
4:15	19

1 John

3:11	2
4:7	2
4:8	9, 12

Index of Composers, Arrangers, and Sources

"Agincourt Song, The" (1415), 21
Beethoven, Ludwig van, 3, 26, 35, 44
Caniadau y Cyssegr (1839), 12, 14
Croft, William, 18, 39
Dutch melody, 37
Dykes, John Bacchus, 20
Elvey, George Job, 50
Emerson, L. O., 10, 11
English Hymnal, The (1906), 5, 6, 40
Evans' *Hymnau a Thonau* (1865), 5, 6, 40
Ferris, Theodore P., 45
Foundery Collection, The (1742), 22
Gaelic melody, 32
Gesangbuch der Herzogl. Wirtembergischen Katholischen Hofkapelle (1784), 49
Genevan Psalter (1551), 47
German melody, 19
Goss, John, 17, 19, 36, 41
Grotenhuis, Dale, 32
Haydn, Franz Joseph, 31, 38
Haydn, Johann Michael, 13
Hebrew melody, 51
Hodges, Edward, 3, 26, 35, 44

Hughes, John, 8
Kocher, Conrad, 1, 9
Mendelssohn, Felix, 25
Messiter, Arthur H., 52
Nares, James, 22
Parry, C. Hubert H., 24
Prichard, Rowland Hugh, 2, 33, 34
Röntgen, Julius, 37
Schlesische Volkslieder (1842), 46
Scott-Gatty, Alfred, 48
Sheppard, Franklin L., 7
Silesian folk melody, 46
Smart, Henry Thomas, 27, 29, 30
Stralsund *Ernewerten Gesangbuch* (1665), 42
Supplement to the New Version of the Psalms, A (1708), 18, 39
Taylor, Cyril Vincent, 43
Traditional Welsh melody, 10, 11, 16
Welsh folk melody, 5, 6, 12, 14, 40
Willcox, John H., 4
Williams, Ralph Vaughan, 28
Wyeth's *Repository of Sacred Music* (1813), 23
Zundel, John, 15

Alphabetical Index of Tunes

Asterisk (*) denotes music under copyright, requiring permission to reprint.
Please see notes under each hymn.

*Abbot's Leigh.....................................43
Amsterdam..22
Ar hyd y nos 10, 11
Armageddon.....................................19
Austrian Hymn 31, 38
Beecher...15
Blaenhafren.....................................16
*Bunessan 32
Consolation......................................25
Crusaders' Hymn 46
Cwm Rhondda 9
Deo gracias......................................21
Diademata..50
Dix 1, 9
Dominus regit me 20
Ellacombe 49
Faben 4
Hanover..39
Hyfrydol....................................2, 33, 34

Hymn to Joy 3, 26, 35, 44
In Babilone...37
*King's Weston 28
Lauda anima 17, 36, 41
Leoni...51
Llangloffan 5, 6, 40
Lobe den Herren..............................42
Lyons 13
Marion...52
Nettleton 23
Regent Square.......................27, 29, 30
Rustington...24
St. Anne 18
St. Denio 12, 14
Terra beata...7
Toulon 47
Welwyn..48
*Weymouth 45

Metrical Index of Tunes

D (Double) indicates that the meter is repeated.

55 54 D
Bunessan 32

56 85 58
Crusaders' Hymn 46

65 65 D
King's Weston 28

65 65 65 D
Armageddon 19

66 84 D
Leoni .51

76 76 D
Llangloffan 5, 6, 40

76 76 77 76
Amsterdam 22

77 77 77
Dix 1, 9

84 84 88 84
Ar hyd y nos 10, 11

87 87
Dominus regit me 20

87 87 D
Abbot's Leigh 43
Austrian Hymn 31, 38
Beecher 15
Blaenhafren 16
Faben 4
Hyfrydol 2, 33, 34
Hymn to Joy 3, 26, 35, 44
In Babilone 37
Nettleton 23
Rustington 24

87 87 87
Lauda anima 17, 36, 41
Regent Square 27, 29, 30

87 87 877
Cwm Rhondda 8

10 10 10 10
Toulon 47

10 10 11 11
Hanover 39
Lyons .13

11 10 11 10
Consolation 25
Welwyn 48

11 11 11 11
St. Denio 12, 14

14 14 4 7 8
Lobe den Herren 42

CM (Common Meter = 86 86)
St. Anne 18

CMD (Common Meter Double)
Ellacombe 49
Weymouth 45

LM (Long Meter = 88 88)
Deo Gracias 21

SM with Refrain (Short Meter = 66 86)
Marion 52

SMD [Short Meter Double]
Diademata 50
Terra Beata 7

Index of First Lines

All praise to God for word
   and words.....................................18
Christ has come, salvation bringing....4
Christ, you give us living water.........31
Creator God, you build
   your church...............................49
Creator of mountains.........................14
God beyond us, God within us..........35
God is here in word and action.........24
"God is love," the Bible teaches........10
God of all communication.................16
God of beauty, truth, and grace...........1
God of beginnings..............................46
God of days and years and eons........44
God of life, in Christ you lead us......43
God of our years 42
God of time and space and thought ..22
Gracious God of all creation..............11
Gratefully offer talents and service ...32
Holy God of all creation.....................27
Holy God, we name you 28
"I am who I am, I will be who
   I will" 12
"I am who I am"—our living God's
   name 13
Justice is a journey onward...............38
Loving God of all creation 26
Loving Spirit, great Creator...............33
Loving Spirit, our Creator 30
Oh Dios de lo creado (O God of all
   creation) 6
O faithful God of years long past.......45

O give God the praise for friendships
   that last......................................39
O God in Christ, you call us into
   mission......................................25
O God of all creation 5
O God of earth and altar 40
O God, you build the church 51
O God, you call to service day
   by day 47
O gracious God, by whom the church
   is founded 48
Open the doors for Christ! 50
"Peace to you"—these words
   of Jesus 37
Planting seeds of faith and trust..........9
Praise the God who formed and
   loved us.....................................41
Rejoice! Our loving God 52
Seeking to be faithful servants 29
Sing, my soul, in praise unending 8
Sing we now of peace with justice.....36
Sovereign God of all creation 34
Sovereign God of every creature 3
The Lord's my Shepherd 20
We remember with thanksgiving.......23
We sing our praise to God 7
We will sing a song of women...........19
When, in awe of God's creation...........2
Word of God in human language 15
Words are tools of peace
   and justice 17
Your word, O God, a sharpened
   blade 21